Insights You Need from Harvard Business Review

Business is changing. Will you adapt or be left behind?

Get up to speed and deepen your understanding of the topics that are shaping your company's future with the **Insights You Need from Harvard Business Review** series. Featuring HBR's smartest thinking on fast-moving issues—blockchain, cybersecurity, AI, and more—each book provides the foundational introduction and practical case studies your organization needs to compete today and collects the best research, interviews, and analysis to get it ready for tomorrow.

You can't afford to ignore how these issues will transform the landscape of business and society. The Insights You Need series will help you grasp these critical ideas—and prepare you and your company for the future.

Books in the series include:

Agile

Artificial Intelligence

Blockchain

Cybersecurity

Monopolies and Tech Giants

Strategic Analytics

Insights You Need from
Harvard
Business
Review

BLOCKCHAIN

Insights You Need from
**Harvard
Business
Review**

BLOCKCHAIN

Harvard Business Review Press

Boston, Massachusetts

Copyright 2019 Harvard Business School Publishing Corporation
All rights reserved
Printed in the United States of America

10 9 8 7 6 5 4 3 2 1

No part of this publication may be reproduced, stored in or introduced into a retrieval system, or transmitted, in any form, or by any means (electronic, mechanical, photocopying, recording, or otherwise), without the prior permission of the publisher. Requests for permission should be directed to permissions@harvardbusiness.org, or mailed to Permissions, Harvard Business School Publishing, 60 Harvard Way, Boston, Massachusetts 02163.

The web addresses referenced in this book were live and correct at the time of the book's publication but may be subject to change.

Library of Congress Cataloging-in-Publication Data

Title: Blockchain : the insights you need from Harvard Business Review.
Other titles: Blockchain (Harvard Business Review Press) |
    Insights you need from Harvard Business Review.
Description: Boston, Massachusetts : Harvard Business Review Press,
    [2019] | Series: The insights you need from Harvard Business Review
Identifiers: LCCN 2019011989 | ISBN 9781633697911 (pbk.)
Subjects: LCSH: Blockchains (Databases) | Data encryption
    (Computer science) | Electronic commerce. | Financial institutions—
    Technological innovations.
Classification: LCC HG1710 .B57 2019 | DDC 658/.0557—dc23
    LC record available at https://lccn.loc.gov/2019011989

ISBN: 978-1-63369-791-1
eISBN: 978-1-63369-792-8

The paper used in this publication meets the requirements of the American National Standard for Permanence of Paper for Publications and Documents in Libraries and Archives Z39.48-1992

Contents

Section 2

Blockchain and Business

Section 3

The Future of Blockchain

Contents

Introduction

BLOCKCHAIN AND THE DATA INTEGRITY REVOLUTION

by Catherine Tucker

While the dizzying evolution of the internet has transformed how we access data and communicate, advances in data integrity and storage have limped along. We can use the internet to instantaneously pinpoint an obscure eatery in Borneo, watch cat videos, or share our views worldwide. But even with the advent of cloud storage technologies, data still gets lost, corrupted, censored, accidentally deleted, hacked, stolen, and destroyed.

Blockchain could eliminate all of these problems. Pioneered in 2008 as a method of verifying cryptocurrency transactions, blockchain consists of a time-stamped, append-only series of blocks of immutable data that is not owned by any single entity. Once a *block* of data is added to the *chain* using cryptography, it can't be removed or modified. Bad actors can't change it. Censors can't remove it. Hackers can't steal what's already been shared. It might be as revolutionary for data integrity and recording as the internet has been for data access.

Better data integrity brings new possibilities. So many business decisions rest on knowing that the data we have actually reflects reality. Take, for example, supply chain: If it were possible, by reviewing a blockchain, to know with certainty that inventory was in a particular place, or arrived or left at a particular time, the cost of verifying its presence would steeply decline. And since these time-stamped transaction records couldn't be manipulated, the likelihood of fraud would drop just as sharply. In so many other industries and functions, blockchain could reduce frictions and shrink bureaucracy to the point where entirely new business models are possible. This book will help you understand what will change, when, and how to prepare.

As a professor at MIT who focuses on the digital economy and as a cofounder of the MIT crypto-economics lab, I spend a lot of time researching how blockchain will affect industry. Blockchain's impact may be slow-moving, but it could ultimately be staggering. Decades may pass before the ramifications of profound new technologies and innovations emerge, and the changes they bring tend not to happen where one might expect. Volta invented the electric battery in 1800, but the development of one that was useful for industrial applications took at least sixty years. After the dot-com bust in 2000, it would have been easy to conclude that the internet held limited potential as a way to sell goods.

Now, with the bursting of the bitcoin bubble and the high-profile stumbles of several blockchain-based startups, some people are going to make similar mistakes. Don't write off blockchain, and don't ignore it because it seems too complicated—misjudging the pivotal moment we are living in could leave your business struggling to catch up. How many companies that underestimated the internet would like to do the year 2000 over again if they could?

Blockchain: The Insights You Need from Harvard Business Review will tell you what you need to know now and will help you better predict how it will affect your business and industry. It will help nontechnical leaders, including executives, board members, and managers in any role, get up to speed. The book is divided into three sections:

- **Understanding Blockchain** is a deep dive into what blockchain is, covering its history, its current trajectory, and its design, and what it can and cannot do.

- **Blockchain and Business** looks at how business is using blockchain today, thinking about finance, payments, supply chains, marketing, and the creative industry.

- **The Future of Blockchain** explores blockchain's power to affect notions of privacy, surveillance, government regulation, and environmental sustainability.

Throughout the book, ask yourself several important questions to better understand how blockchain could help (or disrupt) your business, industry, or society as a whole:

1. Could this outcome have happened without blockchain technology? What value is blockchain technology really adding here?

2. Is the true value of blockchain that the data placed on the blockchain has more integrity, or is the primary value derived from the fact that the data structure is decentralized and no one owns the data?

3. Which firms' business models are most at risk from blockchain? Is it banks, insurance companies, digital platforms like Google, or something else that no one has spotted yet?

4. Will governments adopt blockchain? Will they use it for currency, for record keeping, or for additional purposes? What would be the unique consequences of replacing older technologies with blockchain-based systems in the governmental context?

5. Since no one owns it, who will be the ultimate beneficiary of blockchain? Incumbents or upstarts, companies or people, people who want privacy or people who don't, governments or dissidents?

At this early stage of blockchain adoption, we can acknowledge that even as we can't yet be sure how blockchain technology will change society, we shouldn't sit back and watch transformation happen without us. The insights in this volume sketch out how major industries, governments, marketing practices, and investment patterns could change substantially once data integrity has leaped forward. Use them to prepare yourself and your company for the promising blockchain future.

Section 1

UNDERSTANDING BLOCKCHAIN

THE TRUTH ABOUT BLOCKCHAIN

by Marco Iansiti and Karim R. Lakhani

ontracts, transactions, and the records of them are among the defining structures in our economic, legal, and political systems. They protect assets and set organizational boundaries. They establish and verify identities and chronicle events. They govern interactions among nations, organizations, communities, and individuals. They guide managerial and social action. And yet these critical tools and the bureaucracies formed to manage them have not kept up with the economy's digital transformation. They're like a rush-hour gridlock trapping a Formula 1 race car. In a digital world, the way

How Blockchain Works

Here are five basic principles underlying the technology.

1. **Distributed database.** Each party on a blockchain has access to the entire database and its complete history. No single party controls the data or the information. Every party can verify the records of its transaction partners directly, without an intermediary.

2. **Peer-to-peer transmission.** Communication occurs directly between peers instead of through a central node. Each node stores and forwards information to all other nodes.

3. **Transparency with pseudonymity.** Every transaction and its associated value are visible to anyone with access to the system. Each node, or user, on a blockchain has a unique 30-plus-character alphanumeric address that identifies it. Users can choose to remain anonymous

we regulate and maintain administrative control has to change.

Blockchain promises to solve this problem. The technology at the heart of bitcoin and other virtual currencies, blockchain is an open, distributed ledger or provide proof of their identity to others. Transactions occur between blockchain addresses.

4. **Irreversibility of records.** Once a transaction is entered in the database and the accounts are updated, the records cannot be altered, because they're linked to every transaction record that came before them (hence the term "chain"). Various computational algorithms and approaches are deployed to ensure that the recording on the database is permanent, chronologically ordered, and available to all others on the network.

5. **Computational logic.** The digital nature of the ledger means that blockchain transactions can be tied to computational logic and in essence programmed. So users can set up algorithms and rules that automatically trigger transactions between nodes.

that can record transactions between two parties efficiently and in a verifiable and permanent way. The ledger itself can also be programmed to trigger transactions automatically. (See the sidebar "How Blockchain Works.")

With blockchain, we can imagine a world in which contracts are embedded in digital code and stored in transparent, shared databases, where they are protected from deletion, tampering, and revision. In this world every agreement, every process, every task, and every payment would have a digital record and signature that could be identified, validated, stored, and shared. Intermediaries like lawyers, brokers, and bankers might no longer be necessary. Individuals, organizations, machines, and algorithms would freely transact and interact with one another with little friction. This is the immense potential of blockchain.

Indeed, virtually everyone has heard the claim that blockchain will revolutionize business and redefine companies and economies. Although we share the enthusiasm for its potential, we worry about the hype. It's not just security issues (such as the 2014 collapse of one bitcoin exchange and the more recent hacks of others) that concern us. Our experience studying technological innovation tells us that if there's to be a blockchain revolution, many barriers—technological, governance, organizational, and even societal—will have to fall. It would be a mistake to rush headlong into blockchain innovation without understanding how it is likely to take hold.

True blockchain-led transformation of business and government, we believe, is still many years away. That's because blockchain is not a "disruptive" technology, which can attack a traditional business model with a lower-cost solution and overtake incumbent firms quickly. Blockchain is a *foundational* technology: It has the potential to create new foundations for our economic and social systems. But while the impact will be enormous, it will take decades for blockchain to seep into our economic and social infrastructure. The process of adoption will be gradual and steady, not sudden, as waves of technological and institutional change gain momentum. That insight and its strategic implications are what we'll explore in this article.

Patterns of Technology Adoption

Before jumping into blockchain strategy and investment, let's reflect on what we know about technology adoption and, in particular, the transformation process typical of other foundational technologies. One of the most relevant examples is distributed computer networking technology, seen in the adoption of TCP/IP (transmission control protocol/internet protocol), which laid the groundwork for the development of the internet.

Introduced in 1972, TCP/IP first gained traction in a *single-use* case: as the basis for email among the researchers on ARPANET, the U.S. Department of Defense precursor to the commercial internet. Before TCP/IP, telecommunications architecture was based on "circuit switching," in which connections between two parties or machines had to be preestablished and sustained throughout an exchange. To ensure that any two nodes could communicate, telecom service providers and equipment manufacturers had invested billions in building dedicated lines.

TCP/IP turned that model on its head. The new protocol transmitted information by digitizing it and breaking it up into very small packets, each including address information. Once released into the network, the packets could take any route to the recipient. Smart sending and receiving nodes at the network's edges could disassemble and reassemble the packets and interpret the encoded data. There was no need for dedicated private lines or massive infrastructure. TCP/IP created an open, shared public network without any central authority or party responsible for its maintenance and improvement.

Traditional telecommunications and computing sectors looked on TCP/IP with skepticism. Few imagined that robust data, messaging, voice, and video connections could be established on the new architecture or that the associated system could be secure and scale up. But during the late 1980s and 1990s, a growing number of firms, such as Sun, NeXT, Hewlett-Packard, and Silicon Graphics, used TCP/IP, in part to create *localized* private networks within organizations. To do so, they developed building blocks and tools that broadened its use beyond email, gradually replacing more-traditional local network technologies and standards. As organizations adopted these building blocks and tools, they saw dramatic gains in productivity.

TCP/IP burst into broad public use with the advent of the World Wide Web in the mid-1990s. New technology companies quickly emerged to provide the "plumbing"— the hardware, software, and services needed to connect to the now-public network and exchange information. Netscape commercialized browsers, web servers, and other tools and components that aided the development and adoption of internet services and applications. Sun drove the development of Java, the application-programming language. As information on the web grew exponentially, Infoseek, Excite, AltaVista, and Yahoo were born to guide users around it.

Once this basic infrastructure gained critical mass, a new generation of companies took advantage of low-cost connectivity by creating internet services that were compelling *substitutes* for existing businesses. CNET moved news online. Amazon offered more books for sale than any bookshop. Priceline and Expedia made it easier to buy airline tickets and brought unprecedented transparency to the process. The ability of these newcomers to get extensive reach at relatively low cost put significant pressure on traditional businesses like newspapers and brick-and-mortar retailers.

Relying on broad internet connectivity, the next wave of companies created novel, *transformative* applications that fundamentally changed the way businesses created and captured value. These companies were built on a new peer-to-peer architecture and generated value by coordinating distributed networks of users. Think of how eBay changed online retail through auctions, Napster changed the music industry, Skype changed telecommunications, and Google, which exploited user-generated links to provide more relevant results, changed web search.

Ultimately, it took more than 30 years for TCP/IP to move through all the phases—single use, localized use, substitution, and transformation—and reshape the economy. Today more than half the world's most valuable public companies have internet-driven, platform-based business models. The very foundations of our economy have changed. Physical scale and unique intellectual property no longer confer unbeatable advantages; increasingly, the economic leaders are enterprises that act as "keystones," proactively organizing, influencing, and coordinating widespread networks of communities, users, and organizations.

The New Architecture

Blockchain—a peer-to-peer network that sits on top of the internet—was introduced in October 2008 as part of a proposal for bitcoin, a virtual currency system that eschewed a central authority for issuing currency, transferring ownership, and confirming transactions. Bitcoin is the first application of blockchain technology.

The parallels between blockchain and TCP/IP are clear. Just as email enabled bilateral messaging, bitcoin enables bilateral financial transactions. The development and maintenance of blockchain is open, distributed, and shared—just like TCP/IP's. A team of volunteers around the world maintains the core software. And just like email, bitcoin first caught on with an enthusiastic but relatively small community.

TCP/IP unlocked new economic value by dramatically lowering the cost of connections. Similarly, blockchain could dramatically reduce the cost of transactions. It has the potential to become the system of record for all transactions. If that happens, the economy will once again undergo a radical shift, as new, blockchain-based sources of influence and control emerge. Consider how business works now. Keeping ongoing records of transactions is a core function of any business. Those records track past actions and performance and guide planning for the future. They provide a view not only of how the organization works internally but also of the organization's outside relationships. Every organization keeps its own records, and they're private. Many organizations have no master ledger of all their activities; instead records are distributed across internal units and functions. The problem is, reconciling transactions across individual and private ledgers takes a lot of time and is prone to error.

For example, a typical stock transaction can be executed within microseconds, often without human intervention. However, the settlement—the ownership transfer of the stock—can take as long as a week. That's because the parties have no access to each other's ledgers and can't automatically verify that the assets are in fact owned and can be transferred. Instead a series of intermediaries act as guarantors of assets as the record of the transaction traverses organizations and the ledgers are individually updated.

In a blockchain system, the ledger is replicated in a large number of identical databases, each hosted and maintained by an interested party. When changes are entered in one copy, all the other copies are simultaneously updated. So as transactions occur, records of the value and assets exchanged are permanently entered in all ledgers. There is no need for third-party intermediaries to verify or transfer ownership. If a stock transaction took place on a blockchain-based system, it would be settled within seconds, securely and verifiably. (The infamous hacks that have hit bitcoin exchanges exposed weaknesses not in the blockchain itself but in separate systems linked to parties using the blockchain.)

A Framework for Blockchain Adoption

If bitcoin is like early email, is blockchain decades from reaching its full potential? In our view the answer is a qualified yes. We can't predict exactly how many years the transformation will take, but we can guess which kinds of applications will gain traction first and how blockchain's broad acceptance will eventually come about.

In our analysis, history suggests that two dimensions affect how a foundational technology and its business use cases evolve. The first is novelty—the degree to which an application is new to the world. The more novel it is, the more effort will be required to ensure that users understand what problems it solves. The second dimension is complexity, represented by the level of ecosystem coordination involved—the number and diversity of parties that need to work together to produce value with the technology. For example, a social network with just one member is of little use; a social network is worthwhile only when many of your own connections have signed on to it. Other users of the application must be brought on board to generate value for all participants. The same will be true for many blockchain applications. And, as the scale and impact of those applications increase, their adoption will require significant institutional change.

We've developed a framework that maps innovations against these two contextual dimensions, dividing them into quadrants. (See figure 1-1.) Each quadrant represents a stage of technology development. Identifying which one a blockchain innovation falls into will help executives understand the types of challenges it presents, the level of collaboration and consensus it needs, and the legislative and regulatory efforts it will require. The map will also suggest what kind of processes and infrastructure must be established to facilitate the innovation's adoption. Managers can use it to assess the state of blockchain development in any industry, as well as to evaluate strategic investments in their own blockchain capabilities.

Single use

The low-novelty and low-coordination applications in the first quadrant create better, less costly, highly focused solutions. Email, a cheap alternative to phone calls, faxes, and snail mail, was a single-use application for TCP/IP (even though its value rose with the number of users). Bitcoin, too, falls into this quadrant. Even in its early days, bitcoin offered immediate value to the few people who used it simply as an alternative payment method. (You can think of it as a complex email that transfers not just information but also actual value.) At the end of 2016 the value of bitcoin transactions was expected to hit $92 billion. That's still a rounding error compared with the $411 trillion in total global payments, but bitcoin is growing fast and increasingly important in contexts such as instant payments and foreign currency and asset trading, where the present financial system has limitations.

Localization

The second quadrant comprises innovations that are relatively high in novelty but need only a limited number of users to create immediate value, so it's still relatively easy

FIGURE 1-1

How foundational technologies take hold

The adoption of foundational technologies typically happens in four phases. Each phase is defined by the novelty of the applications and the complexity of the coordination efforts needed to make them workable. Applications low in novelty and complexity gain acceptance first. Applications high in novelty and complexity take decades to evolve but can transform the economy. TCP/IP technology, introduced on ARPANET in 1972, has already reached the transformation phase, but blockchain applications (in white) are in their early days.

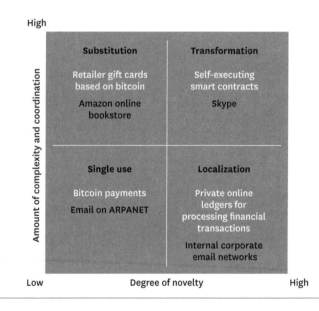

to promote their adoption. If blockchain follows the path network technologies took in business, we can expect blockchain innovations to build on single-use applications to create local private networks on which multiple organizations are connected through a distributed ledger.

Much of the initial private blockchain-based development is taking place in the financial services sector, often within small networks of firms, so the coordination requirements are relatively modest. Nasdaq is working with Chain.com, one of many blockchain infrastructure providers, to offer technology for processing and validating financial transactions. Bank of America, JPMorgan, the New York Stock Exchange, Fidelity Investments, and Standard Chartered are testing blockchain technology as a replacement for paper-based and manual transaction processing in such areas as trade finance, foreign exchange, cross-border settlement, and securities settlement. The Bank of Canada is testing a digital currency called CAD-coin for interbank transfers. We anticipate a proliferation of private blockchains that serve specific purposes for various industries.

Substitution

The third quadrant contains applications that are relatively low in novelty because they build on existing single-use and localized applications but are high in coordination needs because they involve broader and increasingly public uses. These innovations aim to replace entire ways of doing business. They face high barriers to adoption, however; not only do they require more coordination but the processes they hope to replace may be full-blown and deeply embedded within organizations and institutions. Examples of substitutes include cryptocurrencies— new, fully formed currency systems that have grown out of the simple bitcoin payment technology. The critical difference is that a cryptocurrency requires every party that does monetary transactions to adopt it, challenging governments and institutions that have long handled and overseen such transactions. Consumers also have to change their behavior and understand how to implement the new functional capability of the cryptocurrency.

A recent experiment at MIT highlights the challenges ahead for digital currency systems. In 2014 the MIT Bitcoin Club provided each of MIT's 4,494 undergraduates with $100 in bitcoin. Interestingly, 30% of the students did not even sign up for the free money, and 20% of the sign-ups converted the bitcoin to cash within a few weeks. Even the technically savvy had a tough time understanding how or where to use bitcoin.

One of the most ambitious substitute blockchain applications is Stellar, a nonprofit that aims to bring affordable financial services, including banking, micropayments, and remittances, to people who've never had access to them. Stellar offers its own virtual currency, lumens, and also allows users to retain on its system a range of assets, including other currencies, telephone minutes, and data credits. Stellar initially focused on Africa, particularly Nigeria, the largest economy there. It has seen significant adoption among its target population and proved its cost-effectiveness. But its future is by no means certain, because the ecosystem coordination challenges are high. Although grassroots adoption has demonstrated the viability of Stellar, to become a banking standard, it will need to influence government policy and persuade central banks and large organizations to use it. That could take years of concerted effort.

Transformation

Into the last quadrant fall completely novel applications that, if successful, could change the very nature of economic, social, and political systems. They involve coordinating the activity of many actors and gaining institutional agreement on standards and processes. Their adoption will require major social, legal, and political change.

"Smart contracts" may be the most transformative blockchain application at the moment. These automate payments and the transfer of currency or other assets as negotiated conditions are met. For example, a smart contract might send a payment to a supplier as soon as a shipment is delivered. A firm could signal via blockchain that a particular good has been received—or the product could have GPS functionality, which would automatically log a location update that, in turn, triggered a payment. We've already seen a few early experiments with such self-executing contracts in the areas of venture funding, banking, and digital rights management.

The implications are fascinating. Firms are built on contracts, from incorporation to buyer-supplier relationships to employee relations. If contracts are automated, then what will happen to traditional firm structures, processes, and intermediaries like lawyers and accountants? And what about managers? Their roles would all radically change. Before we get too excited here, though, let's remember that we are decades away from the widespread adoption of smart contracts. They cannot be effective, for instance, without institutional buy-in. A tremendous degree of coordination and clarity on how smart contracts are designed, verified, implemented, and enforced will be required. We believe the institutions responsible for those daunting tasks will take a long time to evolve. And the technology challenges—especially security—are daunting.

Guiding Your Approach to Blockchain Investment

How should executives think about blockchain for their own organizations? Our framework can help companies identify the right opportunities.

For most, the easiest place to start is single-use applications, which minimize risk because they aren't new and involve little coordination with third parties. One strategy is to add bitcoin as a payment mechanism. The infrastructure and market for bitcoin are already well developed, and adopting the virtual currency will force a variety of functions, including IT, finance, accounting, sales, and marketing, to build blockchain capabilities. Another low-risk approach is to use blockchain internally as a database for applications like managing physical and digital assets, recording internal transactions, and verifying identities. This may be an especially useful solution for companies struggling to reconcile multiple internal databases. Testing out single-use applications will help organizations develop the skills they need for more-advanced applications. And thanks to the emergence of cloud-based blockchain services from both startups and large platforms like Amazon and Microsoft, experimentation is getting easier all the time.

Localized applications are a natural next step for companies. We're seeing a lot of investment in private blockchain networks right now, and the projects involved seem poised for real short-term impact. Financial services companies, for example, are finding that the private blockchain networks they've set up with a limited number of trusted counterparties can significantly reduce transaction costs.

Organizations can also tackle specific problems in transactions across boundaries with localized applications. Companies are already using blockchain to track items through complex supply chains, for instance. This is happening in the diamond industry, where gems are being traced from mines to consumers. The technology for such experiments is now available off-the-shelf.

Developing substitute applications requires careful planning, since existing solutions may be difficult to dislodge. One way to go may be to focus on replacements that won't require end users to change their behavior much but present alternatives to expensive or unattractive solutions. To get traction, substitutes must deliver functionality as good as a traditional solution's and must be easy for the ecosystem to absorb and adopt. First Data's foray into blockchain-based gift cards is a good example of a well-considered substitute. Retailers that offer them to consumers can dramatically lower costs per transaction and enhance security by using blockchain to track the flows of currency within accounts—without relying on external payment processors. These new gift cards even allow transfers of balances and transaction capability between merchants via the common ledger.

Transformative applications are still far away. But it makes sense to evaluate their possibilities now and invest in developing technology that can enable them. They will be most powerful when tied to a new business model in which the logic of value creation and capture departs from existing approaches. Such business models are hard to adopt but can unlock future growth for companies.

Consider how law firms will have to change to make smart contracts viable. They'll need to develop new expertise in software and blockchain programming. They'll probably also have to rethink their hourly payment model and entertain the idea of charging transaction or hosting fees for contracts, to name just two possible approaches. Whatever tack they take, executives must be sure they understand and have tested the business model implications before making any switch.

Transformative scenarios will take off last, but they will also deliver enormous value. Two areas where they could have a profound impact: large-scale public identity systems for such functions as passport control, and algorithm-driven decision making in the prevention of money laundering and in complex financial transactions that involve many parties. We expect these applications won't reach broad adoption and critical mass for at least another decade and probably more.

Transformative applications will also give rise to new platform-level players that will coordinate and govern the new ecosystems. These will be the Googles and Facebooks of the next generation. It will require patience to realize such opportunities. Though it may be premature to start making significant investments in them now, developing the required foundations for them—tools and standards—is still worthwhile.

Conclusion

In addition to providing a good template for blockchain's adoption, TCP/IP has most likely smoothed the way for it. TCP/IP has become ubiquitous, and blockchain applications are being built on top of the digital data, communication, and computation infrastructure, which lowers the cost of experimentation and will allow new use cases to emerge rapidly.

With our framework, executives can figure out where to start building their organizational capabilities for blockchain today. They need to ensure that their staffs learn about blockchain, to develop company-specific applications across the quadrants we've identified, and to invest in blockchain infrastructure.

But given the time horizons, barriers to adoption, and sheer complexity involved in getting to TCP/IP levels of acceptance, executives should think carefully about the risks involved in experimenting with blockchain. Clearly, starting small is a good way to develop the know-how to think bigger. But the level of investment should depend on the context of the company and the industry. Financial services companies are already well down the road to blockchain adoption. Manufacturing is not.

No matter what the context, there's a strong possibility that blockchain will affect your business. The very big question is when.

TAKEAWAYS

Blockchain will revolutionize business, but it's going to take decades to do so. This is because it's a foundational technology that will require broad technological, regulatory, and social coordination to implement.

✓ Blockchain, the technology at the heart of bitcoin and other virtual currencies, is an open, distributed ledger that can efficiently, verifiably, and permanently record transactions between two parties.

✓ The adoption of TCP/IP suggests blockchain will follow a fairly predictable pattern of development, so it's not too early for businesses to start planning.

✓ With a 2×2 framework that maps the novelty and complexity of blockchain applications, managers can assess the state of blockchain development in any industry, and evaluate strategic investments in their own blockchain capabilities.

✓ Organizations can develop their blockchain capabilities by starting with single-use applications and then, over time, move into more complex, novel, and ultimately transformative ones.

Adapted from an article in Harvard Business Review, January–February 2017 (product #R1701J).

A BRIEF HISTORY OF BLOCKCHAIN

by Vinay Gupta

Many of the technologies we now take for granted were quiet revolutions in their time. Just think about how much smartphones have changed the way we live and work. It used to be that when people were out of the office, they were *gone*, because a telephone was tied to a place, not to a person. Now we have global nomads building new businesses straight from their phones. And, think, smartphones have been around for merely a decade.

We're now in the midst of another quiet revolution: blockchain, a distributed database that maintains

a continuously growing list of ordered records, called
"blocks." Consider what's happened in just the past 10 years:

- The first major blockchain innovation was bitcoin,
  a digital currency experiment. Bitcoin is used by
  millions of people for payments, including a large
  and growing remittances market.

- The second innovation was called blockchain, which
  was essentially the realization that the underlying
  technology that operated bitcoin could be separated
  from the currency and used for all kinds of other
  interorganizational cooperation. Almost every major
  financial institution in the world is using blockchain
  or doing blockchain research at the moment.

- The third innovation was called the "smart contract," embodied in a second-generation blockchain
  system called Ethereum, which built little computer
  programs directly into blockchain that allowed
  financial instruments, like loans or bonds, to be
  represented, rather than only the cash-like tokens of
  the bitcoin. The Ethereum smart contract platform
  now has a market cap in the billions of dollars, with
  hundreds of projects headed toward the market.

- The fourth major innovation, the current cutting
  edge of blockchain thinking, is called "proof of

stake." Current generation blockchains are secured by "proof of work," in which the group with the largest total computing power makes the decisions. These groups are called "miners" and operate vast data centers to provide this security, in exchange for cryptocurrency payments. The new systems do away with these data centers, replacing them with complex financial instruments, for a similar or even higher degree of security.

- The fifth major innovation on the horizon is called blockchain scaling. Right now, in the blockchain world, every computer in the network processes every transaction. This is slow. A scaled blockchain accelerates the process, without sacrificing security, by figuring out how many computers are necessary to validate each transaction and dividing up the work efficiently. To manage this without compromising the legendary security and robustness of blockchain is a difficult problem, but not an intractable one. A scaled blockchain is expected to be fast enough to power the internet of things and go head-to-head with the major payment middlemen (Visa and SWIFT) of the banking world.

This innovation landscape represents just 10 years of work by an elite group of computer scientists, cryptographers, and mathematicians. As the full potential of these breakthroughs hits society, things are sure to get a little weird. Self-driving cars and drones will use blockchains to pay for services like charging stations and landing pads. International currency transfers will go from taking days to an hour, and then to a few minutes, with a higher degree of reliability than the current system has been able to manage.

These changes, and others, represent a pervasive lowering of transaction costs. When transaction costs drop past invisible thresholds, there will be sudden, dramatic, hard-to-predict aggregations and disaggregations of existing business models. For example, auctions used to be narrow and local, rather than universal and global, as they are now on sites like eBay. As the costs of reaching people dropped, there was a sudden change in the system. Blockchain is reasonably expected to trigger as many of these cascades as e-commerce has done since it was invented, in the late 1990s.

Predicting what direction it will all take is hard. Did anybody see social media coming? Who would have predicted that clicking on our friends' faces would replace time spent in front of the TV? Predictors usually overestimate how fast things will happen and underestimate the long-term impacts. But the sense of scale inside the blockchain industry is that the changes coming will be "as large as the original invention of the internet," and this may not be overstated. What we can predict is that as blockchain matures and more people catch on to this new mode of collaboration, it will extend into everything from supply chains to provably fair internet dating (eliminating the possibility of fake profiles and other underhanded techniques). And given how far blockchain has come in 10 years, perhaps the future could indeed arrive sooner than any of us think.

Until the late 1990s it was impossible to process a credit card securely on the internet—e-commerce simply did not exist. How fast could blockchain bring about another revolutionary change? Consider that Dubai's blockchain strategy (disclosure: I designed it) is to issue all government documents on blockchain by 2020, with substantial initial projects going live three years earlier. The Internet of Agreements concept presented at the World Government Summit builds on this strategy to envision a substantial transformation of global trade, using blockchains to smooth out some of the bumps caused by Brexit and the U.S. withdrawal from the Trans-Pacific Partnership. These ambitious agendas will have to be proven in practice, but the expectation in Dubai is that cost savings and innovation benefits will more than justify the cost of experimentation. As Mariana Mazzucato writes in *The Entrepreneurial State*, the cutting edge of innovation, particularly in infrastructure, is often in the hands of the state, and that seems destined to be true in the blockchain space.

TAKEAWAYS

The blockchain landscape has grown from bitcoin to smart contracts to proof-of-stake systems in just 10 years. These developments all point to a pervasive lowering of transaction costs in the future.

✓ When transaction costs drop past certain thresholds, there will be sudden, dramatic, hard-to-predict aggregations and disaggregations of existing business models.

✓ Predictors usually overestimate how fast technologies will be adopted and underestimate their long-term impacts. Even so, the thinking in the blockchain industry is that the changes coming may be as large as the original invention of the internet.

✓ Governments and NGOs are already a driving force in blockchain innovation.

Adapted from content posted on hbr.org, originally published February 28, 2017 (product #H03HW6).

THE BLOCKCHAIN WILL DO TO THE FINANCIAL SYSTEM WHAT THE INTERNET DID TO MEDIA

by Joichi Ito, Neha Narula, and Robleh Ali

E ven years into the deployment of the internet, many believed that it was still a fad. Of course, the internet has since become a major influence on our lives, from how we buy goods and services, to the ways we socialize with friends, to the Arab Spring, to the 2016 U.S.

presidential election. Yet, in the 1990s, the mainstream press scoffed when Nicholas Negroponte predicted that most of us would soon be reading our news online rather than from a newspaper.

Fast forward two decades: Will we soon be seeing a similar impact from cryptocurrencies and blockchains? There are certainly many parallels. Like the internet, cryptocurrencies such as bitcoin are driven by advances in core technologies along with a new, open architecture— the bitcoin blockchain. Like the internet, this technology is designed to be decentralized, with "layers," where each layer is defined by an interoperable open protocol on top of which companies, as well as individuals, can build products and services. Like the internet, in the early stages of development there are many competing technologies, so it's important to specify *which* blockchain you're talking about. And, like the internet, blockchain technology is strongest when everyone is using the same network, so in the future we might all be talking about "the" blockchain.

The internet and its layers took decades to develop, with each technical layer unlocking an explosion of creative and entrepreneurial activity. Early on, Ethernet standardized the way in which computers transmitted bits over wires, and companies such as 3Com were able to build empires on their network switching products.

The TCP/IP protocol was used to address and control how packets of data were routed between computers. Cisco built products like network routers, capitalizing on that protocol, and by March 2000 Cisco was the most valuable company in the world. In 1989 Tim Berners-Lee developed HTTP, another open, permissionless protocol, and the web enabled businesses such as eBay, Google, and Amazon.

The Killer App for Blockchains

But here's one major difference: The early internet was noncommercial, developed initially through defense funding and used primarily to connect research institutions and universities. It wasn't designed to make money, but rather to develop the most robust and effective way to build a network. This initial lack of commercial players and interests was critical—it allowed the formation of a network architecture that shared resources in a way that would not have occurred in a market-driven system.

The killer app for the early internet was email; it's what drove adoption and strengthened the network. Bitcoin is the killer app for blockchain. Bitcoin drives adoption of its underlying blockchain, and its strong technical community and robust code review process make it the most secure and reliable of the various blockchains. Like email, it's likely that some form of bitcoin will persist. But blockchain will also support a variety of other applications, including smart contracts, asset registries, and many new types of transactions that will go beyond financial and legal uses.

We might best understand bitcoin as a microcosm of how a new, decentralized, and automated financial system could work. While its current capabilities are still limited (for example, there's a low transaction volume when compared to conventional payment systems), it offers a compelling vision of a possible future because the code describes both a regulatory and an economic system. For example, transactions must satisfy certain rules before they can be accepted into the bitcoin blockchain. Instead of writing rules and appointing a regulator to monitor for breaches, which is how the current financial system works, bitcoin's code sets the rules and the network checks for compliance. If a transaction breaks the rules (for example, if the digital signatures don't tally), it is rejected by the network. Even bitcoin's "monetary policy" is written into its code: New money is issued every 10 minutes, and the supply is limited so there will only ever be 21 million bitcoins, a hard money rule similar to the gold standard (that is, a system in which the money supply is fixed to a commodity and not determined by government).

This is not to say the choices bitcoin currently offers are perfect. In fact, many economists disagree with bitcoin's hard money rule, and lawyers argue that regulation through code alone is inflexible and doesn't permit any role for useful discretion. What cannot be disputed, however, is that bitcoin is real, and it works. People ascribe real economic value to bitcoins. "Miners," who maintain the bitcoin blockchain, and "wallet providers," who write the software people use to transact in bitcoin, follow the rules without exception. Its blockchain has remained resilient to attack, and it supports a robust, if basic, payment system. This opportunity to extend the use of blockchain to remake the financial system unnerves and enthralls in equal measure.

Too Much Too Soon?

Unfortunately, the exuberance of fintech investors is way ahead of the development of the technology. We're often seeing so-called blockchains that are not really innovative, but instead are merely databases, which have existed for decades, calling themselves blockchains to jump on the buzzword bandwagon.

There were many pre-internet players, for example telecom operators and cable companies trying to provide interactive multimedia over their networks, but none could generate enough traction to create names that you would remember. We may be seeing a similar trend for blockchain technology. The landscape is a combination of incumbent financial institutions making incremental improvements and new startups building on top of rapidly changing infrastructure, hoping that the quicksand will harden before they run out of runway.

In the case of cryptocurrencies, we're seeing far more aggressive investments of venture capital than we did for the internet during similar early stages of development. This excessive interest by investors and businesses makes cryptocurrencies fundamentally different from the internet because they haven't had several decades of relative obscurity where noncommercial researchers could fiddle, experiment, iterate on, and rethink the architecture. This is one reason why the work that we're doing at the Digital Currency Initiative at the MIT Media Lab is so important: It is one of the few places where a substantial effort is being made to work on the technology and infrastructure clear of financial interests and motivations. This is critical.

The existing financial system is very complex at the moment, and that complexity creates risk. A new decentralized financial system made possible with cryptocurrencies could be much simpler by removing layers of intermediation. It could help insure against risk, and by moving money in different ways could open up the possibility for different types of financial products. Cryptocurrencies could open up the financial system to people who are currently excluded, lower barriers to entry, and enable greater competition. Regulators could remake the financial system by rethinking the best way to achieve policy goals, without diluting standards. We could also have an opportunity to reduce systemic risk: Like users, regulators suffer from opacity. Research shows that making the system more transparent reduces intermediation chains and costs to users of the financial system.

Conclusion

The primary use and even the values of the people using new technologies and infrastructure tend to change drastically as these technologies mature. This will certainly be true for blockchain technology.

Bitcoin was first created as a response to the 2008 financial crisis. The originating community had a strong libertarian and antiestablishment spin that, in many ways, was similar to the free-software culture, with its strong anticommercial values. However, it is likely that, just as Linux is now embedded in almost every kind of commercial application or service, many of the ultimate use cases of blockchain could become standard fare for established players like large companies, governments, and central banks.

Similarly, many view blockchain technology and fintech as merely a new technology for delivery—maybe something akin to CD-ROMs. In fact, it is more likely to do to the financial system and regulation what the internet has done to media companies and advertising firms. Such a fundamental restructuring of a core part of the economy is a big challenge to incumbent firms that make their living from it. Preparing for these changes means investing in research and experimentation. Those who do so will be well placed to thrive in the new, emerging financial system.

TAKEAWAYS

It's common to look to the emergence and mainstreaming of the internet to predict the future of blockchain. But the early internet was noncommercial, and it enjoyed decades of relative obscurity during which researchers could experiment, iterate on, and rethink its architecture.

Blockchain, however, began to attract interest from investors mere years after its invention.

✓ Fintech investors' exuberance for blockchain is ahead of the technology's level of development. Many entrepreneurs are jumping on the bandwagon applying the buzzword "blockchain" to databases that aren't actually blockchain-based.

✓ The world's existing financial system is very complex, and that complexity creates risk. A new decentralized, cryptocurrency-based financial system could help reduce risk, open up the financial system to people who are currently excluded, and enable greater competition.

Adapted from content posted on hbr.org, originally published March 8, 2017 (product #H03I8K).

4

WHO CONTROLS THE BLOCKCHAIN?

by Patrick Murck

B lockchain networks tend to support principles, like open access and permissionless use, that should be familiar to proponents of the early internet. To protect this vision from political pressure and regulatory interference, blockchain networks rely on a decentralized infrastructure that can't be controlled by any one person or group. Unlike political regulation, blockchain governance is not emergent from the community. Rather, it is ex ante, encoded in the protocols and processes as an integral part of the original network architecture. To be a part of a community supporting a blockchain is to accept the rules of the network as they were originally established.

In a blockchain transaction, you don't have to trust your counterpart to perform their obligations or properly record transactional data, since these processes are standardized and automated, but you do have to trust that the code and the network will function as you expect. And just how immutable are blockchain ledger entries if the network becomes politicized? As it turns out, not very.

Consider the case of The DAO. Short for *decentralized autonomous organization*, a DAO is software designed to manage the fiduciary obligations of holding and disbursing blockchain assets without any human involvement. The code that was developed for (confusingly named) The DAO application was called a "smart contract," and ran as a DAO application on top of the Ethereum blockchain. The DAO issued tokens through its smart contract and traded them for Ethereum's blockchain tokens, which are called ether. This token sale was done through a widely marketed crowdfunding campaign, raising more than $150 million in ether value.

The original vision of the Ethereum creators was that computer code should, quite literally, be treated as law in their community and serve as replacement for legal agreements and regulation. The DAO creators embraced this vision and noted that participants should look exclusively to the application's code as dispositive on all matters. The code was the contract and the law for The DAO. Unfortunately, The DAO's smart contract was flawed: It allowed a DAO token holder who exploited a bug in the code to siphon off one-third of the value held in the application (roughly $50 million) to their own account. This withdrawal of funds, while unexpected, did not violate either Ethereum's or The DAO's rules, naive as they may have been. Nor does it appear to have violated any laws.

But, at the end of the day, too many Ethereum community members, including some of its most prominent leaders, suffered losses, having traded their ether for DAO tokens. They felt that action had to be taken to reverse their losses. The Ethereum leadership was able to coordinate with the network stakeholders to create a so-called "hard fork," a permanent split of the Ethereum blockchain, so that control of the siphoned-off funds would be shifted to a group of trusted leaders.

This hard fork created a new Ethereum blockchain and was labeled a bailout by critics. The new Ethereum blockchain selectively rolled back losses only for those Ethereum blockchain token holders who had unwisely exchanged those tokens for The DAO application tokens. If you happened to lose your ether tokens in any other way, whether through market manipulation or through another hack, the rigid "code as law" doctrine still applied—and you were out of luck.

For some members of the community, the decision to hard fork was a wanton violation of the community's core principles, akin to burning down the house to roast the pig. In protest, they decided to keep running the original Ethereum blockchain unadulterated, and thus there are now two Ethereum networks. Somewhat confusingly, the old Ethereum network has been rebranded as "Ethereum Classic"; the new network retained the original name, Ethereum.

Blockchain fabulists may claim that smart contract applications like The DAO's will displace lawyers and disrupt the legal industry. But as this incident amply demonstrated, the reality is that smart contracts have proven to be neither smart nor, for that matter, enforceable agreements. Blockchain is truly an innovative approach to governance for networks and machines. But we must resist the temptation to anthropomorphize code and misapply machine governance to social systems. Code is law for machines, law is code for people. When we mix up these concepts, we wind up with situations like The DAO.

Consider some of the controversy surrounding bitcoin. First, understand that on the bitcoin blockchain, power is meant to be distributed among all the stakeholders in the community. None of these stakeholders should have any greater influence or power than any other to change the terms of the bitcoin protocol. They are interdependent and incentivized to cooperate in conserving the extant network rules. Any change to the network rules requires coordination and consensus among all of the stakeholders. So when bitcoin software developers began debating about how to increase network capacity, the discussion devolved into a multistakeholder melee that was dubbed a "governance crisis" by the popular media. Some of the developers wanted to incorporate changes to the bitcoin codebase that would not be backward compatible, and thus would split the network into multiple blockchains—a hard fork.

The majority of bitcoin developers have opposed hardfork scaling proposals in favor of a more conservative approach that assures the continuity of a single bitcoin blockchain. Other stakeholders have begun to view this process as obstructionist, and populist campaigns have sprung up to route around it. But despite much Sturm und Drang, these efforts to alter bitcoin's power structure and circumvent bitcoin developer consensus have thus far failed. For many in the community, bitcoin's ability to resist such populist campaigns demonstrates the success of the blockchain's governance structure and shows that the "governance crisis" is a false narrative.

As a blockchain community grows, it becomes increasingly more difficult for stakeholders to reach a consensus on changing network rules. This is by design and reinforces the original principles of the blockchain's creators. To change the rules is to split the network, creating a new blockchain and a new community. Blockchain networks resist political governance because they are governed by everyone who participants in them, and by no one in particular.

The power of blockchain technology is that it can algorithmically enforce private agreements and community principles at a global scale by shifting the cost of trust and coordination to the network. This is what allows blockchains to create new markets where they couldn't exist before, whether for political or for economic reasons. To do this, we have to be able to trust the blockchain, and to trust that no one controls it.

TAKEAWAYS

Blockchain networks tend to support idealistic principles such as open access and permissionless use. To protect this vision from political pressure and regulatory interference, blockchain networks rely on a decentralized infrastructure that can't be controlled by any one person or group.

✓ In a blockchain transaction, you don't have to trust that your counterpart will perform their obligations—but you do have to trust that the code and the network will function as you expect.

✓ In practice, blockchain ledger entries are not immutable if enough network participants want to change them. The case of The DAO, in which a flaw in code allowed a user to siphon off $50 million worth of value into their own account, shows that "code is law" isn't simple to apply in the real world.

✓ As a blockchain community grows, it becomes increasingly more difficult for stakeholders to reach a consensus on changing network rules. Blockchain networks resist political governance because they are governed by everyone who participants in them, and by no one in particular.

Adapted from content posted on hbr.org, originally published April 19, 2017 (product #H03LUX).

5

HOW SAFE ARE BLOCKCHAINS? IT DEPENDS

by Allison Berke

Blockchain, the distributed ledger technology underlying bitcoin, may prove to be far more valuable than the currency it supports. But it's only as valuable as it is secure. As we begin to put distributed ledger technology into practice, it's important to make sure that the initial conditions we're establishing aren't setting us up for security issues later on.

To understand the inherent security risks in blockchain technology, it's important to understand the difference between public and private blockchains.

Bitcoin relies on a public blockchain, a system of recording transactions that allows anyone to read or write transactions. Anyone can aggregate and publish those transactions, provided they can show that a sufficient amount of effort went into doing so, which they can demonstrate by solving a difficult cryptographic puzzle. The process by which a network of nodes confirms the record of previously verified transactions, and by which it verifies new transactions, is known as a consensus protocol. In the bitcoin system, because no user is implicitly trusted to verify transactions, all users follow an algorithm that verifies transactions by committing software and hardware resources to solving a problem by brute force (that is, by solving the cryptographic puzzle). The user who reaches the solution first is rewarded, and each new solution, along with the transactions that were used to verify it, forms the basis for the next problem to be solved.

This decentralization and relative freedom of access has led to some unexpected consequences: Because anyone can read and write transactions, bitcoin transactions have fueled black market trading. Because the consensus protocol is energy consuming, the majority of users operate in countries with cheap electricity, leading to network centralization and the possibility of collusion, and making the network vulnerable to changes in policy on electricity subsidies. Both of these trends have led to an increased interest in private blockchains, which could ultimately give businesses a greater degree of control.

Primarily used in financial contexts, private blockchains give their operators control over who can read the ledger of verified transactions, who can submit transactions, and who can verify them. The applications for private blockchains include a variety of markets in which multiple parties wish to participate simultaneously but do not fully trust one another. For example, private blockchain systems supporting land and physical asset registries, commodities trading, and private equity distribution are all being tested. As these systems develop and evolve, they, too, may encounter unexpected consequences, some of which will have repercussions for the security of the system and the assets it manages or stores. As in software and product development, considering security at an early stage alleviates the difficulty of making fundamental changes to a product to address a security flaw later on.

Security Starts with Network Architecture

One of the first decisions to make when establishing a private blockchain is about the network architecture of the system. Blockchains achieve consensus on their ledger, the list of verified transactions, through communication, and communication is required to write and approve new transactions. This communication occurs between nodes, each of which maintains a copy of the ledger and informs the other nodes of new information: newly submitted or newly verified transactions. Private blockchain operators can control who is allowed to operate a node, as well as how those nodes are connected; a node with more connections will receive information faster. Likewise, nodes may be required to maintain a certain number of connections to be considered active. A node that restricts the transmission of information, or transmits incorrect information, must be identifiable and circumventable to maintain the integrity of the system. A private blockchain underlying commodities trading may grant more-central positions in the network to established trading partners and may require new nodes to maintain a connection to one of these central nodes as a security measure to ensure it behaves as expected.

Another security concern in the establishment of network architecture is how to treat uncommunicative or intermittently active nodes. Nodes may go offline for innocuous reasons, but the network must be structured to function (to obtain consensus on previously verified transactions and to correctly verify new transactions) without the offline nodes, and it must be able to quickly bring these nodes back up to speed if they return.

Consensus Protocols and Access Permissions in Public vs. Private Blockchains

The process used to get consensus (verifying transactions through problem solving) is purposely designed to take time, currently around 10 minutes. Transactions are not considered fully verified for about one to two hours, after which point they are sufficiently "deep" enough in the ledger that introducing a competing version of the ledger, known as a fork, would be computationally expensive. This delay is both a vulnerability of the system, in that a transaction that initially seems to be verified may later lose that status, and a significant obstacle to the use of bitcoin-based systems for fast-paced transactions, such as financial trading.

In a private blockchain, by contrast, operators can choose to permit only certain nodes to perform the verification process, and these trusted parties would be responsible for communicating newly verified transactions to the rest of the network. The responsibility for securing access to these nodes, and for determining when and for whom to expand the set of trusted parties, would be a security decision made by the blockchain system operator.

Transaction Reversibility and Asset Security in Public vs. Private Blockchains

While blockchain transactions can be used to store data, the primary motivation for bitcoin transactions is the exchange of bitcoin itself. Each bitcoin transaction includes unique text strings that are associated with the bitcoins being exchanged. Similarly, other blockchain systems record the possession of assets or shares involved in a transaction. In the bitcoin system, ownership is demonstrated through the use of a private key (a long number generated by an algorithm designed to provide a random and unique output) that is linked to a payment, and despite the value of these keys, like any data, they can be stolen or lost, just like cash. These thefts are not a failure of the security of bitcoin, but of personal security; the thefts are the result of storing a private key insecurely. Some estimates put the value of lost bitcoins in the billions.

Private blockchain operators therefore must decide how to resolve the problem of lost identification credentials, particularly for systems that manage physical assets. Even if no one can prove ownership of a barrel of oil, the barrel will need to reside somewhere. Bitcoin currently provides no recourse for those who have lost their private keys; similarly, stolen bitcoins are nearly impossible to recover, as transactions submitted with stolen keys appear to a verifying node to be indistinguishable from legitimate transactions.

Private blockchain owners will have to make decisions about whether, and under what circumstances, to reverse a verified transaction, particularly if that transaction can be shown to be a theft. Transaction reversal can undermine confidence in the fairness and impartiality of the system, but a system that permits extensive losses as a result of the exploitation of bugs will lose users. This is illustrated by the case of The DAO, a code-based venture capital fund designed to run on Ethereum, a public blockchain-based platform. Security vulnerabilities in the code operating The DAO led to financial losses that required Ethereum's developers to make changes to the Ethereum protocol itself, even though The DAO's vulnerabilities were not the fault of the Ethereum protocol. The decision to make these changes was controversial and underscores the idea that both public and private blockchain developers should consider circumstances under which they would face a similar decision.

Weighing the Rewards

The benefits offered by a private blockchain—faster transaction verification and network communication, the ability to fix errors and reverse transactions, and the ability to restrict access and reduce the likelihood of outsider attacks—may cause prospective users to be wary of the system. The need for a blockchain system at all presupposes a degree of mistrust, or at least an acknowledgment that all users' incentives may not be aligned. Developers who work to maintain public blockchain systems like bitcoin still rely on individual users to adopt any changes they propose, which serves to ensure that changes are only adopted if they are in the interest of the entire system. The operators of a private blockchain, on the other hand, may choose to unilaterally deploy changes with which some users disagree. To ensure both the security and the utility of a private blockchain system, operators must consider the recourse available to users who disagree with changes to the system's rules or are slow to adopt the new rules. The number of operating systems currently running without the latest patch is a strong indication that even uncontroversial changes will not be adopted quickly.

While the risks of building a financial market or other infrastructure on a public blockchain may give a new entrant pause, private blockchains offer a degree of control over both participant behavior and the transaction verification process. The use of a blockchain-based system is a signal of the transparency and usability of that system, which are bolstered by the early consideration of the system's security. Just as a business will decide which of its systems are better hosted on a more secure private intranet or on the internet, but will likely use both, systems requiring fast transactions, the possibility of transaction reversal, and central control over transaction verification will be better suited for private blockchains, while those that benefit from widespread participation, transparency, and third-party verification will flourish on a public blockchain.

Blockchains are only as valuable as they are secure. When establishing a blockchain network, it's important to make sure that the initial conditions are set up so they don't cause security issues later on.

- ✓ Just as businesses decide which of their systems are better hosted on the internet or more secure private intranets, they will face choices about which of their applications are a better fit for public or private blockchains.

✓ There's a growing interest in private blockchains thanks to the business risks surrounding public blockchains (such as bitcoin), ranging from black market trading to concerns surrounding collusion.

✓ Applications for private blockchains include markets in which multiple parties do not fully trust one another, including physical asset registries, commodities trading, and private equity distribution.

✓ Public blockchains provide no recourse for dealing with lost or stolen private keys. Private blockchains' owners will have to make decisions about whether, and under what circumstances, to reverse a transaction, particularly if that transaction can be shown to be a theft.

Adapted from content posted on hbr.org, originally published March 7, 2017 (product #H03IAZ).

6

WHAT BLOCKCHAIN CAN'T DO

by Catherine Tucker and Christian Catalani

Blockchain technology has the potential to do amazing things. It can provide an immutable, digital audit trail of transactions and can be used to cheaply verify the integrity of data. It can help businesses and individuals agree, on a global scale, about the true state of affairs within a market without relying on a costly intermediary.

This is achieved through a clever combination of economic incentives and cryptography, and ensures that at any point in time, digital records reflect the true consensus among the key stakeholders involved. When it comes to sharing digital records and assets, it can therefore replace the need for trust between players, or the need for a central authority to verify and maintain the records of transactions.

However, when assessing blockchain business models, it is useful to understand what blockchain can't do.

Think about the problem of tracking babies within a hospital ward and beyond. This is a very serious problem. The consequences of a baby being mistaken for another baby can be horrendous. Therefore, storing records that contain a baby's current location in a way that makes these data points immutable and verifiable seems like a great use of blockchain technology.

But there is a big problem with using blockchain to solve such a problem. The digital records may be immutable and verifiable, but how does someone know which digital record is attached to which baby? To link an entry on the blockchain to an actual, real-life baby, we need to give the baby a physical identifier through a physical tag, or in a more futuristic world, a small chip or digital genome record that links the baby to its digital record. And this is where blockchain falls down. It can't help with this process and can't verify that perhaps the most important step of verification is happening correctly.

At the interface between the offline world and its digital representation, the usefulness of the technology still critically depends on trusted intermediaries to effectively bridge the last mile between a digital record and a physical individual, business, device, or event. In our example, the technology would have to rely on humans to correctly and honestly implement the match between baby and digital record. And if humans get that wrong or manipulate the data when it is entered, in a system where records are believed ex post as having integrity, this can have serious negative consequences.

On the other hand, if the link between an individual and their medical record is successfully established and the last-mile problem is solved, then a blockchain can be used not only to ensure data integrity but also to give individuals control over how their medical data is used (for academic research, a fitness app, or commercial drug development, for example).

There are other parallel examples. Within marketing, one issue that often comes up is that a pair of eyeballs that an advertiser is paying for may not actually belong to the person they're supposed to. The advertiser might think it's paying to show an ad to a mid-thirties male in the market for a Lamborghini, but the ad might actually be shown to a minivan-driving academic who has no intention of buying another car for kids to wreck but who likes to dream. Or, even worse, a bot could be viewing the ad. Blockchain technology can track which digital identifiers are associated with the viewing of an ad, but it cannot help with verifying humanness or the honesty of a buyer's intentions. Verifying who's actually behind the digital identifier requires offline verification. Verifying the honesty of apparent buying intentions is perhaps beyond any technology we possess today.

On the bright side, blockchain technology can be used to change the relationship between digital content creators, advertisers, and consumers. Advertisers can reward users for their attention by giving them access to exclusive online content they would otherwise have to pay for. Content creators can explore new monetization models that benefit from blockchain's ability to cheaply and effectively settle transactions. While consumers hate micropayments because of the mental costs they involve—micropayments are like a hated "taxi meter" in consumers' heads—this could reshape how paywalls and subscriptions work behind the scenes across different digital properties. Moreover, if we are not worried about verifying a pair of eyeballs' humanness, but instead want to ensure ownership over digital records such as browsing data, then blockchain can work perfectly. One of the issues we face constantly in establishing the economics of privacy is the issue of property rights over data. And blockchain is perfectly positioned to define them.

As the ecosystem around blockchain technology develops, new types of intermediaries will emerge that turn the last-mile problem, of keeping digital records in sync with their offline counterparts, into actual business opportunities. While the technology is early stage, as these key complements mature, blockchain has the potential to fundamentally reshape ownership over digital data, and the digital platforms we use every day.

TAKEAWAYS

When assessing blockchain business models, it is important to understand what blockchain *can't* do. The usefulness of blockchain to many business contexts still depends on trusted intermediaries to effectively bridge the last mile between a digital record and a physical individual, business, device, or event.

✓ For instance, blockchain technology could be used to keep a newborn baby from being mistaken for another newborn baby in a hospital ward. But blockchain technology provides no help in verifying that the right identifier (for instance, a bracelet tag) is applied to the right baby.

✓ As the ecosystem around blockchain technology develops, new business opportunities will emerge around intermediaries that keep digital records in sync with their offline counterparts.

Adapted from content posted on hbr.org, originally published June 28, 2018 (product #H04F3C).

Section 2

BLOCKCHAIN AND BUSINESS

7

HOW BLOCKCHAIN IS CHANGING FINANCE

by Alex Tapscott and Don Tapscott

O ur global financial system moves trillions of dollars a day and serves billions of people. But the system is rife with problems, adding cost through fees and delays, creating friction through redundant and onerous paperwork, and opening up opportunities for fraud and crime. To wit, 45% of financial intermediaries, such as payment networks, stock exchanges, and money transfer services, suffer from economic crime every year; the number is 37% for the entire economy, and only 20% and 27% for the professional services and technology sectors, respectively.[1] It's no small wonder that regulatory costs continue to climb and remain a top concern for bankers. This all adds cost, with consumers ultimately bearing the burden.

It begs the question: Why is our financial system so inefficient? First, because it's antiquated, a kludge of industrial technologies and paper-based processes dressed up in a digital wrapper. Second, because it's centralized, which makes it resistant to change and vulnerable to systems failures and attacks. Third, it's exclusionary, denying billions of people access to basic financial tools. Bankers have largely dodged the sort of creative destruction that, while messy, is critical to economic vitality and progress. But the solution to this innovation logjam has emerged: blockchain.

Blockchain was originally developed as the technology behind cryptocurrencies like bitcoin. A vast, globally distributed ledger running on millions of devices, it is capable of recording anything of value. Money, equities, bonds, titles, deeds, contracts, and virtually all other kinds of assets can be moved and stored securely, privately, and from peer to peer, because trust is established not by powerful intermediaries like banks and governments, but by network consensus, cryptography, collaboration, and clever code. For the first time in human history, two or more parties, be they businesses or individuals who may not even know each other, can forge agreements, make transactions, and build value without relying on intermediaries (such as banks, rating agencies, and government bodies such as the U.S. Department of State) to verify their identities, establish trust, or perform the critical business logic—contracting, clearing, settling, and record-keeping tasks that are foundational to all forms of commerce.

Given the promise and peril of such a disruptive technology, many firms in the financial industry, from banks and insurers to audit and professional service firms, are investing in blockchain solutions. What is driving this deluge of money and interest? Most firms cite opportunities to reduce friction and costs. After all, most financial intermediaries themselves rely on a dizzying, complex, and costly array of intermediaries to run their own operations. Santander, a European bank, put the potential savings at $20 billion a year.[2] Capgemini, a consultancy, estimates that consumers could save up to $16 billion in banking and insurance fees each year through blockchain-based applications.[3]

To be sure, blockchain may enable incumbents such as JPMorgan Chase, Citigroup, and Credit Suisse, all of which are currently investing in the technology, to do more with less, streamline their businesses, and reduce risk in the process. But while an opportunistic viewpoint is advantageous and often necessary, it is rarely sufficient.

After all, how do you cut cost from a business or market whose structure has fundamentally changed? Here, blockchain is a real game changer. By reducing transaction costs among all participants in the economy, blockchain supports models of peer-to-peer mass collaboration that could make many of our existing organizational forms redundant.

For example, consider how new business ventures access growth capital. Traditionally, companies target angel investors in the early stages of a new business, and later look to venture capitalists, eventually culminating in an initial public offering (IPO) on a stock exchange. This industry supports a number of intermediaries, such as investment bankers, exchange operators, auditors, lawyers, and crowdfunding platforms (such as Kickstarter and Indiegogo). Blockchain changes the equation by enabling companies of any size to raise money in a peer-to-peer way, through global distributed share offerings. This new funding mechanism is already transforming the blockchain industry. In 2016 blockchain companies raised $400 million from traditional venture investors and nearly $200 million through what we call initial coin offerings (ICO rather than IPO). These ICOs aren't just new cryptocurrencies masquerading as companies. They represent content and digital rights management platforms (such as SingularDTV), distributed venture funds (such as The DAO, for decentralized autonomous organization), and even new platforms to make investing in ICOs and managing digital assets easy (such as ICONOMI). There is already a deep pipeline of ICOs, such as Cosmos, a unifying technology that will connect every blockchain in the world, which is why it's been dubbed the "internet of blockchains." Others are sure to follow suit.

Incumbents are taking notice. The New York–based venture capital firm Union Square Ventures (USV) broadened its investment strategy so that it could buy ICOs directly. Menlo Park venture capital firm Andreessen Horowitz joined USV in investing in Polychain Capital, a hedge fund that only buys tokens. Blockchain Capital, one of the industry's largest investors, recently announced that it would be raising money for its new fund by issuing tokens by ICO, a first for the industry. And, of course, companies such as Goldman Sachs; Nasdaq, Inc.; and Intercontinental Exchange, the American holding company that owns the New York Stock Exchange, which dominate the IPO and listing business, have been among the largest investors in blockchain ventures.

As with any radically new business model, ICOs have risks. There is little to no regulatory oversight. Due diligence and disclosures can be scant, and some companies that have issued ICOs have gone bust. Caveat emptor is the watchword, and many of the early backers are more punters than funders. But the genie has been unleashed from the bottle. Done right, ICOs can not only improve the efficiency of raising money, lowering the cost of capital for entrepreneurs and investors, but also democratize participation in global capital markets.

If the world of venture capital can change radically in one year, what else can be transformed? Blockchain could upend a number of complex intermediate functions in the industry: identity and reputation, moving value (payments and remittances), storing value (savings), lending and borrowing (credit), trading value (marketplaces like stock exchanges), insurance and risk management, and audit and tax functions.

Is this the end of banking as we know it? That depends on how incumbents react. Blockchain is not an existential threat to those who embrace the new technology paradigm and disrupt from within. The question is, Who in the financial services industry will lead the revolution? Throughout history, leaders of old paradigms have struggled to embrace the new. Why didn't AT&T launch Skype, or Visa create PayPal? CNN could have built Twitter, since it is all about the sound bite. GM or Hertz could have launched Uber; Marriott could have invented Airbnb. The unstoppable force of blockchain technology is barreling down on the infrastructure of modern finance. As with prior paradigm shifts, blockchain will create winners and losers. Personally, we would like the inevitable collision to transform the old money machine into a prosperity platform for all.

Our antiquated financial system is inefficient, vulnerable to attack, exclusionary, and resistant to change. Blockchain could provide solutions to this innovation logjam.

✓ Cryptocurrency allows any two or more parties to forge agreements, make transactions, and build value without relying on intermediaries to verify their identities, establish trust, and perform other administrative tasks.

✓ Blockchain enables companies of any size to raise money in a peer-to-peer, global, distributed way through initial coin offerings (ICOs).

✓ Blockchain could upend a number of complex intermediate functions in the financial industry, but whether this is the end of banking as we know it may depend on how incumbents react. Blockchain is not an existential threat to companies that embrace the new technology paradigm and disrupt from within.

NOTES

1. PricewaterhouseCoopers, "Economic Crime: A Threat to Business Globally," PwC 2014 Economic Crime Survey, https://www.pwc.com/gx/en/financial-services/publications/assets/pwc-gecs-2014-threats-to-the-financial-services-sector.pdf.

2. Yessi Bello Perez, "Santander: Blockchain Tech Can Save Banks $20 Billion a Year," Coindesk, June 16, 2015, https://www.coindesk.com/santander-blockchain-tech-can-save-banks-20-billion-a-year.

3. Saktipada Maity, "Consumers Set to Save Up to Sixteen Billion Dollars on Banking and Insurance Fees Thanks to Blockchain-Based Smart Contracts Says Capgemini Report," Capgemini, October 11, 2016, https://www.capgemini.com/news/consumers-set-to-save-up-to-sixteen-billion-dollars-on-banking-and-insurance-fees-thanks-to/.

Adapted from content posted on hbr.org, originally published March 1, 2017 (product #H03HJK).

8

AS CRYPTOCURRENCIES RISE, WHO NEEDS BANKS?

by Antonio Fatás and Beatrice Weder di Mauro

Do you value bitcoin in dollars or dollars in bitcoin? Few serious economists imagine that the new cryptocurrencies, for all the hype, will make national currencies redundant. By and large they are right, because conventional money actually does a pretty good job. The U.S. dollar and other reserve currencies have historically performed well as a medium of exchange and as a store of value—the two principal functions of a currency. Bitcoin and its derivatives perform poorly on both accounts and will not disrupt money as we know it.

But that doesn't mean that new technologies aren't going to usher in a lot of disruption to the financial system. Traditional economists (and, yes, that label could well describe both of us) often ignore a crucial separation between money (the "what") and the payment technology (the "how"). This confusion originates in the fact that for older forms of money—gold or bank notes—there is no distinction between the "what" and the "how"; you simply pay by handing dollar bills or gold coins to the seller.

Today, however, we pay out physical cash less and less often. Instead, when we transact, we usually transfer digital code in exchange for the good or service we're buying. And it is through the technology that digitizes money that new entrants are challenging the financial system.

We've already seen this sort of change in the developing world, where not everyone has access to a bank account. In East Africa, for example, mobile phone companies leapfrogged banks as payment intermediaries because they made it possible for people to transfer cash-convertible phone credits to each other. That meant that people could use phone credits as a digital medium of exchange and that the payment infrastructure became the mobile network.

Of course, in advanced economies, most consumers have access to a bank account with debit and credit cards, which means that they are already engaging in transfers of digital money. This made traditional banks in the United States and Europe far less vulnerable to disruptive innovators, even though their e-payment technologies may in some cases be clunky and unreliable. What's more, to compete directly with banks in a developed economy, you had to demonstrate that your technology was compatible with the existing infrastructure and pass all the regulatory hurdles to be recognized as a bank.

This is where bitcoin came in. The advantage of cryptocurrencies is not that they are electronic currencies; dollars, euros, yen, and yuan are all e-currencies today. Rather, the advantage is that blockchain technology offers a complete, self-contained alternative to the traditional payment transfer system; it is as if all bitcoin users are banking with the same bank. And because cryptocurrencies were not initially regulated, there was no need to go through any of the regulatory processes to get started as a cryptocurrency bank equivalent.

That's just what two startups did. Circle, founded in 2013, provided a peer-to-peer payment system using bitcoin. Ripple, launched in 2012, provided a cross-border payment system that initially relied on a cryptocurrency (XRP) as the payment vehicle. Since XRP also relies on a blockchain technology (a more efficient one than bit-coin's, in fact), it would also provide a central clearing system.

So what? Traditional banks provide very similar services by relying on real-time gross interbank settlement processes through a central bank. But banks face two difficulties: Changing legacy systems and coordinating across the established payment networks is costly and takes time. And in the case of international transactions, they face the difficulty of managing liquidity pools in different currencies, as there is no central bank of the world. In this environment, a brand-new system based on a cryptocurrency (a "global currency") at first looks like a winning proposition.

The trouble is that using bitcoin and its ilk requires users to cope with another currency, an exchange rate, and all the attendant uncertainty about value, which runs into concerns about the storage value of money. This necessarily limits the appeal of startups like Circle and Ripple—which is precisely why they have moved away from cryptocurrencies and are looking for ways to apply their technology to traditional currencies and link directly with banks and central banks.

Fintech companies in this space will be aided by new regulation, which may prove to be the real disruptor. Both the Open Banking initiative in the U.K. and the PSD2 directive of the European Union now require banks to provide access, through APIs, to customers' accounts. This is a critical change because it enables parties other than the banks holding money to effect transfers: Individuals can use their preferred smartphone app to make payments without having to embrace a world with separate money balances and possibly separate currencies. The app will access the relevant accounts through the APIs, and transactions can be completed.

In effect, the new regulations will enable a separation of the functions of money. Commercial banks may continue to hold our money balances in traditional currencies and make loans to businesses with those balances, but transactions may be intermediated by a separate payment technology, at least in the eye of the final user.

And if we want payment systems to be integrated, is there any need for multiple intermediaries? Why not simply make payment transfer a central bank function instead? If every individual had accounts at the central bank, and these were linked across countries, that would create a centralized ledger for an entire economy, which would certainly increase the speed, safety, and efficiency of payments. Central banks are considering this idea but so far have concluded that the risks to the financial system are very high and the benefits are uncertain.[1] If it happened, though, the financial system would without doubt be profoundly changed.

TAKEAWAYS

The U.S. dollar and other reserve currencies have historically performed well both as a medium of exchange and as a store of value. Cryptocurrencies don't do well at either of these yet, but they're still going to usher in a lot of disruption to the financial system.

✓ People are using cash less and less often, and new entrants that are digitizing money are bypassing the established financial system. In East Africa, for example, mobile phone companies leapfrogged banks as payment intermediaries.

✓ Blockchain has an advantage as a digitized currency because it offers a complete, self-contained alternative to the traditional payment transfer system; it is as if all bitcoin users are banking with the same bank.

✓ Using cryptocurrency presents challenges. Users need to worry about an exchange rate and uncertainty around the storage value of cryptocurrency.

✓ New regulations may enable a separation of the exchange and storage functions of money. Commercial banks may continue to hold our money balances in traditional currencies and make loans to businesses with those balances, but transactions may be intermediated by separate payment technologies.

NOTE

1. Committee on Payments and Market Infrastructures, "Central Bank Digital Currencies," Bank for International Settlements, March 12, 2018, https://www.bis.org/cpmi/publ/d174.htm.

Adapted from content posted on hbr.org, originally published May 7, 2018 (product #H04BB3).

9

GLOBAL SUPPLY CHAINS ARE ABOUT TO GET BETTER, THANKS TO BLOCKCHAIN

by Michael J. Casey and Pindar Wong

W hen an *E. coli* outbreak at Chipotle Mexican Grill outlets left 55 customers ill, in 2015, the news stories, shutdowns, and investigations shattered the restaurant chain's reputation. Sales plummeted, and Chipotle's share price dropped 42%, to a three-year low.

At the heart of the Denver-based company's crisis was the ever-present problem faced by companies that depend on multiple suppliers to deliver parts and ingredients: a lack of transparency and accountability across complex supply chains. Unable to monitor its suppliers in real time, Chipotle could neither prevent the contamination nor contain it in a targeted way after it was discovered.

Now, a slew of startups and corporations are exploring a radical solution to this problem: using a blockchain to transfer title and record permissions and activity logs to track the flow of goods and services between businesses and across borders.

With blockchain technology, the core system that underpins bitcoin, computers of separately owned entities follow a cryptographic protocol to constantly validate updates to a commonly shared ledger. A fundamental advantage of this distributed system, where no single company has control, is that it resolves problems of disclosure and accountability between individuals and institutions whose interests aren't necessarily aligned. Mutually important data can be updated in real time, removing the need for laborious, error-prone reconciliation with each other's internal records. It gives each member of the network far greater and timelier visibility of the total activity.

In a nutshell, this is a global system for mediating trust and selective transparency. Its advocates say it will take the internet's empowering potential to its next level. Although much attention and money has been spent on financial applications of the technology, an equally promising test case lies with global supply chain relationships, whose complexity and diversity of interests pose exactly the kinds of challenges this technology seeks to address. The technology can reveal hitherto hidden information and allows users to attach digital tokens—a unique, negotiable form of digital asset, modeled on bitcoin—to intermediate goods as they progress through the production, shipping, and delivery phases of a supply chain and as title to them passes between different players. This could give businesses far greater flexibility to find markets and price risk by capturing the value that they have invested in the process at any point along the chain. What we end up with are dynamic *demand* chains in place of rigid *supply* chains, resulting in more efficient resource use for all.

Various endeavors have already started. Provenance, a U.K.-based startup, tells prospective clients they can use its blockchain-based technology to "share your product's journey and your business impact on environment and society." Walmart is working with IBM and Tsinghua University, in Beijing, to follow the movement of pork in China with a blockchain. Mining giant BHP

Billiton is using the technology to track mineral analysis done by outside vendors. The startup Everledger has uploaded unique identifying data on a million individual diamonds to a blockchain ledger system to build quality assurances and help jewelers comply with regulations barring "blood diamond" products.

Advances in chip and sensor technology, which can translate data from the automated movement of physical goods, should greatly enhance these emerging blockchain systems. It could be especially powerful when combined with "smart contracts," in which contractual rights and obligations, including the terms for payment and delivery of goods and services, can be automatically executed by an autonomous system that's trusted by all signatories.

But this technology's potential traceability and automation benefits don't just pertain to things; it could also keep human beings in check. Staff and supervisors from different vendors can be granted special, cryptographic permissions, which, when placed into a blockchain environment, would appear as unique, traceable identifiers— preferably encrypted, to protect the employee's personal information. This would allow all members of a supply chain community to monitor the activity of each other's credentialed staff. Chipotle, for example, could see in real time whether a properly credentialed person in a facility owned by one of its beef suppliers is carrying out appropriate sterilization and disinfection procedures.

This kind of provable, transparent credentialing will be especially important for additive manufacturing, which is central to the dynamic, on-demand production model of the so-called Industry 4.0 movement. A team from precision parts manufacturer Moog Inc. has launched a service it calls VeriPart, which seeks to overcome a challenge that the director of its additive manufacturing and innovation unit, James Regenor, described to us in these terms: "How can the maintenance crew on a U.S. aircraft carrier have absolute confidence that the software file they downloaded to 3D print a new part for a fighter jet hasn't been hacked by a foreign adversary?" This underscores one of the most compelling arguments for blockchain technology: Without its solution to the trust problem, the sophisticated, decentralized, internet of things–driven economy that many are projecting might well be impossible.

These potential efficiency improvements, enabled by hitherto unavailable information, suggest blockchain technology could deliver vast savings for companies everywhere. But there are formidable obstacles to overcome first.

One challenge lies in the development and governance of the technology. Ideally, to encourage free access, competition, and open innovation, global supply chains would have the option to anchor to a public blockchain that no entity controls. In other words, data extracted from commercial and production activity would be cryptographically recorded in open ledgers. But, inevitably, private, closed ledgers run by a consortium of companies will also arise, as their members seek to protect market share and profits. Both imperatives pose challenges. For one, achieving global economic capacity for the most significant public blockchains, digital currency service bitcoin and smart contract platform Ethereum, is constrained by divisions in their open-source communities, making it difficult to agree on protocol upgrades. Second, there needs to be interoperability across private and public blockchains, which will require standards and agreements.

Another big obstacle: the law. A complex array of regulations, maritime law, and commercial codes governs rights of ownership and possession along the world's shipping routes and their multiple jurisdictions. Marrying that Old World body of law, and the human-led institutions that manage it, with the digitally defined, dematerialized, automated, and denationalized nature of blockchains and smart contracts will be difficult.

Even before governments can be convinced to support this effort, and to do so in a globally coordinated way, industry must agree on best practices and standards of technology and contract structure across international borders and jurisdictions. In Hong Kong, the Belt and Road blockchain consortium seeks to bring order to this process by adopting internet governance approaches pioneered and tested by ICANN (Internet Corporation for Assigned Names and Numbers), the organization that manages domain names. As an international, private sector–led body, ICANN has already proven itself to be an effective global administrator and adjudicator.

These challenges must be weighed against the demands of a global economy that has experienced challenges since the financial crisis of 2008 and is fueling disintegrating, isolationist forces in the United States and Europe. Any system that promises to counter those trends by removing the intercommercial frictions that curb trade while also enhancing transparency and control for businesses and their customers is inherently worth exploring. It's why an increasing number of investors, businesses, academics, and even governments are starting to view blockchain technology as a much-needed platform for economic renewal.

TAKEAWAYS

A slew of startups and corporations are exploring uses of blockchain throughout the global supply chain to transfer titles, record permissions, and log activities to track and expedite the flow of goods and services between businesses and across borders.

✓ A fundamental advantage of this distributed tracking and management system is that it resolves problems of disclosure and accountability between parties whose interests aren't necessarily aligned. Mutually important data can be updated reliably in real time, removing the need for reconciliation with each other's internal records.

✓ Governance, collaboration, interoperability across private and public blockchains, and legal challenges may present roadblocks to adopting these technologies.

Adapted from content posted on hbr.org, originally published March 13, 2017 (product #H03J07).

WHAT BLOCKCHAIN MEANS FOR THE SHARING ECONOMY

by Primavera De Filippi

L ook at the modus operandi of today's internet giants—such as Google, Facebook, Twitter, Uber, or Airbnb—and you'll notice they have one thing in common: They rely on the contributions of users as a means to generate value within their own platforms. Over the past 20 years the economy has progressively moved away from the traditional model of centralized organizations, where large operators, often with a dominant position, were responsible for providing a service to a group of passive consumers. Today we are moving toward a new model of increasingly decentralized organizations, where large operators are responsible for aggregating the resources of multiple people to provide a service to a much more active group of consumers. This shift marks the advent of a new generation of "dematerialized" organizations that do not require physical offices, assets, or even employees.

The problem with this model is that, in most cases, the value produced by the crowd is not equally redistributed among all those who have contributed to the value production; all of the profits are captured by the large intermediaries who operate the platforms.

Recently, a new technology has emerged that could change this imbalance. Blockchain facilitates the exchange of value in a secure and decentralized manner, without the need for an intermediary.

But the most revolutionary aspect of blockchain technology is that it can run software in a secure and decentralized manner. With a blockchain, software applications no longer need to be deployed on a centralized server: They can be run on a peer-to-peer network that is not controlled by any single party. These blockchain-based applications can be used to coordinate the activities of a large number of individuals, who can organize themselves without the help of a third party. Blockchain technology is ultimately a means for individuals to coordinate common activities, to interact directly with one another, and to govern themselves in a more secure and decentralized manner.

There are already a fair number of applications that have been deployed on a blockchain. Akasha, Steem.io, or Synereo, for instance, are distributed social networks that operate like Facebook, but without a central platform. Instead of relying on a centralized organization to manage the network and stipulate which content should be displayed to whom (often through proprietary algorithms that are not disclosed to the public), these platforms are run in a decentralized manner, aggregating the work of disparate groups of peers, which coordinate themselves, only and exclusively, through a set of code-based rules enshrined in a blockchain. People must pay microfees to post messages onto the network, which will be paid to those who contribute to maintaining and operating the network. Contributors may earn back the fee (plus additional compensation) as their messages spread across the network and are positively evaluated by their peers.

Similarly, OpenBazaar is a decentralized marketplace, much like eBay or Amazon, but operates independently of any intermediary operator. The platform relies on blockchain technology to ensure that buyers and sellers can interact directly with one another, without passing through any centralized middleman. Anyone is free to register a product on the platform, which will become visible to all users connected to the network. Once a buyer agrees to the price for that product, an escrow account is created on the bitcoin blockchain that requires two out of three people (that is, the buyer, the seller, and a potential third-party arbitrator) to agree for the funds to be released (a so-called multisignature account). Once the buyer has sent the payment to the account, the seller ships the product; after receiving the product, the buyer releases the funds from the escrow account. Only if there is an issue between the two does the system require the intervention of a third party (for example, a randomly selected arbitrator) to decide whether to release the payment to the seller or whether to return the money to the buyer.

There are also decentralized carpooling platforms, such as LaZooz or Arcade City, which operate much like Uber, but without a centralized operator. These platforms are governed only by the code deployed on a blockchain-based infrastructure, which is designed to govern peer-to-peer interactions between drivers and users. These platforms rely on a blockchain to reward drivers contributing to the platform with specially designed tokens that represent a share in the platform. The more a driver contributes to the network, the more they will be able to benefit from the success of that platform, and the greater their influence in the governance of that organization.

Blockchain technology thus facilitates the emergence of new forms of organizations, which are not only *dematerialized* but also *decentralized*. These organizations—which have no director or CEO, or any sort of hierarchical structure—are administered, collectively, by all individuals interacting on a blockchain. As such, it is important not to confuse them with the traditional model of crowdsourcing, where people contribute to a platform but do not benefit from the success of that platform. Blockchain technologies can support a much more cooperative form of crowdsourcing—sometimes referred to as "platform cooperativism"—where users qualify both as *contributors* and *shareholders* of the platforms to which they contribute. And since there is no intermediary operator, the value produced within these platforms can be more equally redistributed among those who have contributed to the value creation.

With this new opportunity for increased "cooperativism," we're moving toward a true sharing or collaborative economy—one that is not controlled by a few large intermediary operators, but that is governed *by* and *for* the people.

There's nothing new about that, you might say—haven't we heard these promises before? Wasn't the mainstream deployment of the internet supposed to level the playing field for individuals and small businesses competing against corporate giants? And yet, as time went by, most of the promises and dreams of the early internet days faded away, as giants formed and took control over our digital landscape.

Today we have a new opportunity to fulfill these promises. Blockchain technology makes it possible to replace the model of top-down hierarchical organizations with a system of distributed, bottom-up cooperation. This shift could change the way wealth is distributed in the first place, enabling people to cooperate toward the creation of a common good, while ensuring that everyone will be duly compensated for their efforts and contributions.

Yet nothing should be taken for granted. Just as the internet has evolved from a highly decentralized infrastructure into an increasingly centralized system controlled by only a few large online operators, there is always the risk that giants will eventually form in the blockchain space. We've lost our first window of opportunity with the internet. If we, as a society, really value the concept of a true sharing economy, where the individuals doing the work are fairly rewarded for their efforts, it behooves us all to engage and experiment with this emergent technology, to explore the new opportunities it provides, and to deploy large, successful, community-driven applications that enable us to resist the formation of blockchain giants.

TAKEAWAYS

Today's internet giants—think Facebook, Google, and Twitter—rely on the contributions of their users to generate value within their own platforms. The problem with this model is that most of the value produced by the crowd is captured by the large intermediaries that operate the platforms. Blockchain could change this imbalance.

✓ Blockchain offers an opportunity for increased "cooperativism," where we move toward a true sharing or collaborative economy—one that is not controlled by a few large intermediary operators, but that is governed *by* and *for* the people.

✓ A collaborative economy should not be taken for granted. Just as the internet has evolved from a highly decentralized infrastructure into a system controlled by a few large operators, there is always the risk that giants will eventually form in the blockchain space.

Adapted from content posted on hbr.org, originally published March 15, 2017 (product #H03J7F).

HOW BLOCKCHAIN CAN HELP MARKETERS BUILD BETTER RELATIONSHIPS WITH THEIR CUSTOMERS

by Campbell R. Harvey, Christine Moorman, and Marc Toledo

B lockchain has important implications for market-ing and advertising. But according to The CMO Survey, only 8% of firms rate the use of blockchain in marketing as moderately or very important.[1]

Blockchain technology is not well understood and is subject to a lot of hype. This combination creates a natural barrier to entry and has likely caused marketers to take a wait-and-see approach. However, there are many reasons to invest the time now to understand the technology and begin exploring specific marketing applications for your industry. Like digital platforms, social media, martech, fintech, and numerous other innovations, the spoils of blockchain may go to early adopters that commit to ruthless innovation.

Blockchain's properties—transparency, immutability, and security—make it reliable and trustworthy for applications such as supply chain management, smart contracts, financial reporting, the internet of things, the management of private (for example, medical) information, and, even, electrical grid management. Meanwhile, its transmission model reduces the costs of transactions, enables verification and efficient exchange of ownership, and opens the door to real-time micropayments. It may make it possible for payment frictions to shrink, intermediaries to fade away, and consumers to own and control their personal information. Here, we see the disruptive potential of blockchain on marketing.

The Marketing Impact of Near-Zero Transaction Costs

Financial transactions have considerable costs. Retailers routinely pay credit card companies 3% payment processing fees, while gas stations pay even more. Vendors using eBay and Shopify pay listing and sales fees, and consumers pay transaction fees on payment portals like PayPal. All of these fees increase the cost of goods and are typically passed on to consumers. With the pervasive use of credit cards and debit cards, many merchants have set minimum purchases for their use to avoid having their profitability destroyed by fees.

Blockchain technology allows for near-zero transaction costs—even on microtransactions. Financial corporations like Mastercard and Visa already offer the ability to send money in any local currency over a blockchain rather than by swiping a credit card, taking advantage of the technology's additional layers of security and transparency. On top of that, being able to cut intermediaries and connect directly the banks at both ends of each transaction can avoid most cross-border fees.

There are implications for marketers and advertisers as well. Marketers often try to get access to customer data by paying third parties (like Facebook) to share information. But blockchain could allow merchants to use micropayments to motivate consumers to share personal information—directly, without going through an intermediary. For example, a grocery store chain with a mobile app can pay users $1 for installing the app in their phones, plus an extra $1 if they allow it to enable location tracking. Every time they open the app and spend at least a minute on it, the retailer can pay them a few cents or loyalty points' worth of store credit, up to a maximum per day. During that time, they push deals and special offers to the user. Indeed, user-tailored deals open a legitimate mechanism to deliver personalized prices that are a function of the consumer's profile. This approach has the potential to reduce fraud and minimize inaccurate or incomplete information from customers that currently plague these programs.

In the same way, marketers can enable "smart contracts" (virtual agreements that remove the need for validation, review, or authentication by intermediaries) that users can activate when they subscribe to email newsletters or sign up for a rewards program. Micropayments are deposited directly to the users' wallets whenever they interact with commercial emails—or with ads, which brings us to our next point.

Ending the Google-Facebook Advertising Duopoly

A similar model could be used with website ads by compensating consumers for each page view. A majority of internet users dislike most forms of pop-ups and mobile ads and see online advertisement as intrusive and negatively disruptive.[2] An increasingly common response is to install ad blockers, a trend that is having a major punitive effect on the industry. By 2020, it is estimated that ad-blocking adoption will cost publishers $35 billion.[3]

Blockchain-enabled technology potentially allows marketers to recapture some of that revenue with a different type of model: Marketers pay consumers directly for their attention—and cut out the Google-Facebook layer.

We believe that the Google-Facebook duopoly in digital advertising will soon be threatened by blockchain technology. While keyword-based search will not disappear completely, it will become much less prominent. Eventually, individuals could control their own online profiles and social graphs.

With blockchain technology, companies can bypass today's social media powerhouses by directly interacting with consumers and can share the reward of ad exposure directly with them. In 2016, Google is reported to have generated an average of $73 per active user via ads.[4]

Of course, the $73 is just an average over nearly one billion active users. It is reasonable to expect that Google brings in much more than $1,000 for certain highly valued demographics. Imagine the marketing possibilities when companies can efficiently transfer these values to consumers via willingly consumed advertising enabled via blockchain technology.

Blockchain technology can also verify ad delivery and consumer engagement; avoid ad or email overserving, which angers consumers and demotivates them from buying; and prevent follow-me ads that are no longer relevant (such as when consumers have already made a purchase of the company's or competitor's products).

Ending Marketing Fraud and Spam

Fraud verification via blockchain will also help verify the origin and methodology of marketers. Micropayments will also effectively destroy the current concept of mass phishing spam that dilutes the effectiveness of marketing for everyone.

Some 135 billion spam emails are sent every day, currently accounting for 48% of all emails sent. Spammers receive only one reply for every 12.5 million emails sent. A very small blockchain-enabled payment to the recipient of the email will discourage the spammer by increasing the cost of this activity. It should also help companies identify consumers who are interested in the transaction by their willingness to make this exchange.

Similarly, for the internet, every time a user clicks on a link, there could be a micropayment. In most cases, the user will make a small micropayment (for example, one cent to read a news article). This would defeat the DoS attacks—a type of cyber-attack that involves recruiting bots to hit a website with millions of requests that causes the website to go down or to provide poor response time.

Blockchain could also make it difficult for bots to set up fake social media accounts, flood users with deceptive messages, and steal online advertising dollars from big brands. Online authenticity is literally baked into the blockchain technology. One company that is tackling the problem of social media fraud is Keybase.io, which enables individuals to use blockchain to demonstrate that they are the rightful owners of their various social media accounts. This will make the impact of marketing easier to track and marketing expenditures easier to justify—both are big wins for the profession.

As of 2016, $7.6 billion (or 56% of total display ad dollars) were lost to fraudulent or deceptive activity, a number that is expected to grow to $10.9 billion. By using blockchain technology to track their ads, marketing teams can retain control over all their automation practices, ensure that marketing spending is focused on ROI-generating activities, and directly measure the impact of marketing down to a per-user, per-mail metric. By tying user behavior and micropayments together, blockchain could solve the attribution problem that has bedeviled marketers for decades.

Remonetizing Media Consumption

Blockchain-enabled editorial content will likely allow companies to enhance quality control and copyright protection. For instance, (the reinvented) Kodak has created KODAKOne, which features a digital ledger documenting who owns the rights to individual images, allowing photographers to assert control over their work. Currently, the theft of online content is a pervasive problem, and creators have little recourse to recoup lost monies other than expensive lawsuits. In the future, they will automatically and easily receive payments for content usage.

In addition, the average person who creates viral content, such as much-watched videos or social posts, could receive compensation for every click. (Currently, these creators receive little or no money unless their work is shown on online channels with subscribers.)

In all of these scenarios, content creators are empowered to produce relevant work that is valued proportionally to its success.

Companies like Coupit are getting ready to maximize the impact of that improved content. Coupit's blockchain-based technology allows marketers to become part of loyalty and affiliate programs for opted-in consumers who can trade rewards with each other. Marketers gain visibility and transparency to differentiate between dormant and loyal customers, thereby expanding their strategies to send targeted offers to each group.

Even when a data aggregator or analytics intermediary is necessary, micropayments will allow companies to bypass ad blocking. Individuals will control the amount of personal information they share and will be directly rewarded for ad exposure, and many privacy concerns will be legitimately appeased.

One example of this is Brave, a new web browser created by Brendan Eich, cofounder of the Mozilla project and creator of the JavaScript language. Besides offering new levels of privacy and security, Brave is enabling a blockchain-based system aimed at transforming the relationship between users, advertisers, and content creators. Basic Attention Tokens (BATs) will allow publishers to monetize value-added services and capture some of the growth related to advertising, 73% of which is dominated by Facebook and Google.

Better Results for Companies and for Consumers

As blockchain goes mainstream, all intermediaries will need to adapt their business models. The decision chain will be structurally altered: Individuals will have more control over how they share personal information and how they spend their time interacting with advertisers. Spam and phishing scams will be stopped by their own nature—the more spammers spam, the more unsustainable they become from an economic standpoint. For companies, this could mean higher levels of control over the quality of inbound traffic for all their marketing efforts, as well as a much-needed improved understanding of customers' behavior.

On the other hand, exposure to advertisement will not be imposed without a transactional payment to each affected individual. Consumers will also have an incentive to post an accurate social profile online—detailing what they are interested in—because they will get paid for it. Marketers will be paying consumers directly—not the social media middle layer. When targeting high-value customers, the incentives will be accordingly higher.

Blockchain technology holds the potential for societies to become more trustworthy and empowered, increasing visibility, connecting parties, and rewarding individuals for their contributions to transactions. Marketing and advertising are fundamentally impacted by these changes. Finding ways to design and implement measures to make blockchain-related transformations should be a priority not only for CMOs, but also for all strategic, financial, and technological decision makers. Operationally, companies may be able to build new levels of trust with individuals and, ultimately, connect their products and services with consumers in a manner and scale impossible to achieve without blockchain.

Marketing and technology leaders have the potential to leverage blockchain to reinvent their customer relationships. Early action on this far-reaching technology will put companies in the best position to benefit from what we think will be widespread adoption.

TAKEAWAYS

Blockchain's ability to shrink payment frictions and make intermediaries fade away means it has enormous potential to disrupt marketing.

✓ Blockchain-enabled technology could allow marketers to recapture revenue lost to ad blockers and to disrupt the Google-Facebook advertising duopoly by adopting a new model: paying consumers directly for their attention with micropayments.

✓ Fraud verification via blockchain, paired with a micropayment system, could reduce spam and phishing emails, fix the problem of fake social media accounts, and prevent denial-of-service attacks.

✓ Blockchain could reinforce the ownership and copyright protection of online editorial content, allowing content creators, whether professional or amateur, to be fairly compensated for their creations.

NOTES

1. The CMO Survey, "Highlights and Insights Report," February 2018, https://cmosurvey.org/results/february-2018/.

2. Mimi An, "Why People Block Ads (and What It Means for Marketers and Advertisers)," *Hubspot*, July 13, 2016, https://blog.hubspot.com/news-trends/why-people-block-ads-and-what-it-means-for-marketers-and-advertisers.

3. Jessica Davies, "Uh-oh: Ad Blocking Forecast to Cost $35 Billion by 2020," Digiday, June 7, 2016, https://digiday.com/uk/uh-oh-ad-blocking-forecast-cost-35-billion-2020/.

4. "Google's Average Revenue per Monthly Active User from 1st Quarter 2015 to 4th Quarter 2016 (in U.S. Dollars)," Statista, https://www.statista.com/statistics/306570/google-annualized-advertising-arpu/.

Adapted from content posted on hbr.org, originally published October 1, 2018 (product #H04K0R).

BLOCKCHAIN COULD HELP ARTISTS PROFIT MORE FROM THEIR CREATIVE WORKS

by Don Tapscott and Alex Tapscott

A nyone who follows the cultural industries—art, music, publishing, theater, cinema—knows of the tussles between artists and those who feed off their talents. The traditional food chain in movie-making, for example, is a long one: Between those who create a film and those who pay for it—movie goers, cable subscribers, pay-per-viewers, advertisers, rights licensees, and institutional sponsors such as the National Endowment for the Arts—is a multitude of middlemen: online retailers (Amazon, Walmart), streaming video services (Netflix, YouTube, Hulu), theater venues (Wanda's AMC, Regal, Cinemark), product placement and media agencies (Propaganda GEM, Omnicom's OMD), film producers (Columbia Pictures, Marvel Studios, Disney-Pixar), movie distributors (Sony Pictures, Universal, Warner Bros.), home marketers (Fox, HBO), cable and satellite services (Comcast, DIRECTV), video syndicators (PMI, TVS), film libraries and archives (Eastman House, Getty Images), and talent agencies (WME, CAA, ICM), each with its own contracts and accounting systems. That's a staggeringly long list.

Each of these middlemen takes a cut of the revenues and passes along the rest, with the leftovers typically reaching the artists themselves months later, per the terms of their contracts.

So concentrated is the power in this feeding frenzy that many actors have taken themselves off the menu by launching their own companies within the existing industry model. The same is true in music, too. For example, Grammy-award-winning singer-songwriter Imogen Heap has been a pioneer in the field with the launch of Mycelia, a think-and-do tank whose goal is "to empower a fair, sustainable and vibrant music industry ecosystem involving all online music interaction services," using blockchain. Artlery, a company founded by technologists and artists, is attempting the same thing for physical art such as sculptures and paintings. But for most artists and creators, that's not an option.

Enter blockchain-based platforms and programmable templates called *smart contracts*. Blockchain is a new technology platform, running on millions of devices and open to anyone, where not just information but anything of value—money, titles, and deeds, but also music, art, scientific discoveries, and other intellectual property—can be moved and stored securely and privately, where trust is established not by powerful intermediaries like movie studios, streaming services, banks, or other companies, but rather through mass collaboration and clever code.

Combine this powerful new technology with an artistic community that values inclusion, integrity, transparency in deal making, respect of rights, privacy, security, and fair exchange of value, and you've got yourself a new ecosystem for motion pictures, video games, and other creative pursuits.

"A lot of untapped creative energy is wasted on the practicalities that living in a centralized paradigm foster," writes Zach LeBeau, CEO of SingularDTV, a blockchain-based digital content management and distribution platform. His vision is to decentralize the entertainment industry so that creative individuals can profit from the films, videos, games, and art they help to make. He expects decentralization to "realize a world that utilizes the greatest potential of every person."

LeBeau's vision is not a pipe dream. Various companies are already collaborating on blockchain to develop an ecosystem with artist-friendly features, such as:

- **Value templates** to construct deals that respect the artist as an entrepreneur and equal partner in any venture. LeBeau considers the engine of SingularDTV to be its smart contract system, which continually directs the flow of funding to, and revenues from, projects per the automated terms of agreement.

- **Funding mechanisms** whereby artists can raise venture capital. For example, actor Mitzi Peirone used WeiFund, a blockchain-based crowdsale platform, to fund part of her debut thriller, *Braid*. Unlike Kickstarter or Indiegogo, WeiFund turns supporters into investors who share in the profits, should a film become profitable.

- **Inclusive revenues** that use self-executing smart contracts to divide profits fairly and without delays according to each person's contribution to the creative process. This benefits not just actors, screen-writers, and directors, for example, but also other artists and engineers.

- **Transparent ledgers** distributed on the blockchain so that everyone can see how much revenue a film is generating and who is getting what percentage.

- **Micrometering** and **micromonetizing** functionality to stream the revenues immediately to the artists and contributors, the way a film itself streams to online viewers. For example, filmmakers can monetize their content directly by making it available through Wiper, an encrypted messaging app that comes with a bitcoin wallet. Consumers can view films on their mobile devices in exchange for bitcoin.

- **Usage data analytics** in the hands of artists to attract the right merchandisers and distributors, plan promotions, and crowdfund resources for future creative collaborations with other artists.

- **Digital rights management (DRM)**—that is, the deployment of smart contracts to maximize the value of digital rights in a database. For example, Singu-larDTV represents film, television, and software projects on the blockchain as SNGLS tokens.

- **Piracy protection** through public key infrastructure, which enables artists to exchange their assets securely with consumers over networks. For example, Custos Media Technologies, a South African startup, has deployed the bitcoin blockchain to track media piracy by incentivizing the file-sharing community to police pirated content.

- **Dynamic pricing mechanisms** to experiment with promotions and auction-style schemes that could even tie pay-per-view and advertising rates to the online demand for a film.

- **Reputation systems** that cull data from a token address's transaction history and social media, to create a reputation score for that address. Artists will be able to establish their own credibility as well as that of prospective partners and refrain from doing deals with entities that fall short of reputational standards or lack necessary funding in their accounts.

In this new ecosystem, we see a place for Netflix and YouTube, a place for studio curation, and a place for fan-generated content. The film industry will still need people to sift through the hundreds of millions of hours of video created every day all over the planet. The key point is that the artists themselves will finally be feasting at the center of their own ecosystem, not starving at the edges of many others.

TAKEAWAYS

In the arts and other creative industries, there are often countless intermediaries between creators and consumers. Each of these middlemen takes a cut of the revenues and passes along the rest, with the leftovers typically reaching the artists months later.

✓ Blockchain-based smart contracts could reverse this paradigm to create a new ecosystem for creative pursuits based on inclusion, transparency in deal making, respect of rights, and fair exchange of value.

✓ Various companies are already collaborating on blockchain to develop an ecosystem with artist-friendly features including funding mechanisms, micromonetizing, piracy protection, and reputation systems.

Adapted from content posted on hbr.org, originally published March 22, 2017 (product #H03JVQ).

Section 3

THE FUTURE OF BLOCKCHAIN

DOES YOUR IDEA ACTUALLY REQUIRE BLOCKCHAIN?

by Catherine Tucker and Yudan Pang

O ne of our main jobs when teaching and advising students who are thinking of founding blockchain companies is to get them to question whether or not their idea actually requires it. Data integrity is the main benefit conferred by blockchain technology, and a few questions can help determine whether that's a particular problem for a given business or use case:

1. If the data that my business collects is corrupted, how much do people suffer?

2. Do outsiders (perhaps hackers) have incentives to distort or change the data that my business is based upon?

3. How much does my business depend on other people being able to trust the data on which it is built?

Take, for example, a digital currency—the first use case for blockchain. There, if data is corrupted or distorted by outsiders, people lose real money, and the outsider who corrupts the data gains money, making such attacks plausible and to be feared. Therefore, no one will adopt a digital currency unless they can trust their data will not be corrupted or distorted. In other words, there's at least a plausible reason why you'd want blockchain technology managing currency transactions.

However, all too often blockchain startup ideas don't really need blockchain. Their data really isn't that valuable or unique in a way that gives outsiders sufficient economic incentives to launch attacks to try and corrupt or otherwise change it. That's why a recent use of blockchain technology in China in response to the #MeToo movement is so interesting.

In late 2017, an increasing number of stories were being shared on Chinese social media surrounding sexual harassment and abuse of position in Chinese universities. At first, the movement was called *woyeshi*, the Chinese spelling of "Me Too." The Chinese government and technology platforms made repeated attempts to filter out such stories by censoring a variety of hashtags and keywords that campaigners used on Weibo and WeChat. First, *woyeshi* was censored, and then #MeToo, and finally "Rice Bunny," which has the same pronunciation as "Me Too" in Chinese. As a result, campaigners turned to blockchain technology to record their stories under the name "Every Snowflake." This website simply uses a blockchain ledger process to record stories about sexual harassment.

This is a use case that fulfills the three criteria outlined above. Victims desperately want to not be censored, other parties have a deep interest in censoring them, and people can only find value in stories of discrimination if they have not been censored. "Every Snowflake" is a compelling case where blockchain helped people overcome a real problem of data integrity.

However, this project also highlights some of the challenges of using blockchain technology.

The general weakness of using blockchain lies in its interface with other technologies and the rest of the world (see chapter 6 of this volume for more on blockchain's "last-mile problem"). In this case, the "last-mile" challenge comes from the fact that it is still possible to restrict access to data built on the blockchain—for example, by banning the website that displays it.

Last, perhaps the biggest challenge to our privacy is in the fact that digital data usually lives forever unless someone makes strenuous efforts to delete it. Blockchain is even more extreme; it nearly guarantees the data lives forever. Corrections can't be made. Stories can't be modified. This raises challenges. What do libel suits look like when records can't be deleted from the blockchain? What about the "right to be forgotten" that is built into privacy policy in some countries? In the case of sexual harassment, these aren't just questions of protecting the accused. What if a victim comes to regret making a statement publicly and wants to withdraw it, perhaps to protect their privacy or even their safety?

Nonetheless, "Every Snowflake" hints at the possibilities of blockchain in our post-truth world. Not every interesting idea or business proposal requires the blockchain. But where data integrity is essential, it can be transformative.

TAKEAWAYS

Not every business idea needs blockchain. If data integrity is not critical to your business or use case, blockchain may not be required.

✓ A few questions can help determine how essential data integrity is to your use case: *If the data that my business collects is corrupted, how much do people suffer? Do outsiders have incentives to distort or change the data that my business is based upon? How much does my business depend on other people being able to trust the data on which it is built?* Digital currencies fulfill all three of these characteristics.

✓ A more surprising use case for blockchain is Chinese #MeToo activists using the technology to avoid censorship. This use of blockchain also meets the three criteria above.

✓ This case also presents some of the challenges of blockchain: Immutability and permanence of a blockchain means that corrections can't be made, and stories can't be modified. If a victim comes to regret making a statement publicly and wants to withdraw it, perhaps to protect their privacy or safety, they are not able to.

Adapted from "Chinese Activists Are Using Blockchain to Document #MeToo Stories" on hbr.org, October 30, 2018 (product #H04MNY).

HOW REGULATION COULD HELP CRYPTOCURRENCIES GROW

by Stephen J. Obie and Mark W. Rasmussen

I gnorance may be bliss for some, but ask anyone in commerce or finance, and they will make it abundantly clear: Ignorance is risk. For that reason, U.S. markets embrace reasonable regulation to ensure transparency and fairness. Stocks are regulated by the Securities and Exchange Commission (SEC), commodities by the Commodity Futures Trading Commission (CFTC), and government currency by the Department of the Treasury and the Federal Reserve. But an emergent fourth asset class, cryptocurrencies, has no single regulator, and that is leading to uncertainty and confusion.

In 2018 the SEC announced the appointment of one of the agency's veteran attorneys, Valerie Szczepanik, as associate director of the Division of Corporation Finance and senior adviser for digital assets and innovation. This is a welcome development. As "crypto czar," her job is to rationalize the application of U.S. securities laws to cryptocurrencies and work with other agencies to coordinate regulatory oversight.

That will be easier said than done. But it is vitally important.

Without clear regulations, cryptocurrency innovation in the United States is being stifled. Entrepreneurs sit on the sidelines for fear of innocently running afoul of the law. Investors, meanwhile, hang back because of uncertainty regarding valuations. And the commonweal suffers, as other countries lure innovators away from the United States by creating rules that make their jurisdictions more hospitable to this growing asset class.

Given the regulatory uncertainty, the United States also risks allowing fraudulent purveyors of cryptocurrencies to

This article represents the personal views and opinions of the authors and not necessarily those of the law firm with which they are associated.

drive out the good. To be sure, federal and state enforcement officials have aggressively sought to stamp out fraudulent initial coin offerings (ICOs) and cryptocurrency trading platforms.[1] But without clear and coherent guidelines to attract good actors to the U.S. market, fraudsters might push out the good actors. At least one estimate pegs the frequency of ICO scams to be as high as 80%.

Although still nascent, cryptocurrencies worldwide are nevertheless on the rise, with money raised by issuers in the first half of 2018 exceeding the amounts raised in all of 2017.

Yet the growth of this 21st-century innovation is being hampered in the United States because our regulators are forced to use enforcement tools created decades ago, well before the internet took off, and in some cases even before World War II. Additionally, overlapping oversight by various agencies creates a structural barrier to change and drives up costs for creators of cryptocurrencies. This improvised approach needs to be improved.

The SEC has said that whether securities laws apply to a particular cryptocurrency depends on the "facts and circumstances" of the offering. And it has emphasized that the manner in which cryptocurrencies are sold is key to that analysis. Indeed, it has been relatively rare that promoters have sold cryptocurrencies just so the buyer can purchase a good or service on a fully developed network. Rather, more often the buyer is hoping to realize a return on the instrument based on the work of the promoter, which likely makes it an "investment contract" and thus a security under the 1946 Supreme Court decision in *SEC v. Howey Co.* Looking beyond *Howey,* however, the SEC and the crypto czar could take a few thoughtful steps to promote clarity and innovation in the cryptocurrency market:

- Encourage the formation of a self-regulatory body to promote and enforce standards among the crypto community.

- Convene an interagency working group, including representatives from the crypto community, to harmonize existing regulatory practices and develop a formal U.S. policy on cryptocurrencies.

- In connection with the above, provide public notice of a proposed rule governing cryptocurrencies and take comments from the public. (This was the process used to redefine so-called swap entities after the financial crisis.)

- Officially recognize that the amount of decentralization is an important factor in determining whether a cryptocurrency is a security.

- Go beyond the appointment of a crypto czar. The SEC should follow the lead of the CFTC—which created LabCFTC, an initiative for promoting innovation in fintech—in developing an opportunity for SEC regulators to directly engage with industry to address questions about the application of the securities laws to blockchain technologies before launch.

These steps will help to promote order, consistency, and accountability within the cryptocurrency market without imposing undue burdens. And they will help the United States emerge as a wise leader in the regulation of cryptocurrency, which will spur entrepreneurship and innovation in this country. After all, wisdom—more than ignorance—is a truer form of bliss.

TAKEAWAYS

Cryptocurrencies have no single regulator, and that is leading to uncertainty, confusion, and risk that are slowing development and investment. Entrepreneurs sit on the sidelines for fear of innocently running afoul of the law, and investors hang back because of uncertainty regarding valuations. The U.S. SEC's "crypto czar" should take steps to provide regulatory clarity and support innovation to the cryptocurrency market:

✓ Encourage the formation of a self-regulatory body to promote and enforce standards among the crypto community.

✓ Convene an interagency working group, including representatives from the crypto community, to harmonize existing regulatory practices and develop policies.

✓ Provide public notice of proposed rules governing cryptocurrencies and take comments from the public.

✓ Officially recognize that the amount of decentralization is an important factor in determining whether a cryptocurrency is a security.

✓ Develop an opportunity for SEC regulators to directly engage with industry to address questions about the application of the securities laws to blockchain technologies before launch.

NOTE

1. "Cyber Enforcement Actions," U.S. Securities and Exchange Commission, https://www.sec.gov/spotlight/cybersecurity -enforcement-actions.

Adapted from content posted on hbr.org, originally published July 17, 2018 (product #H04FZP).

15

USING BLOCKCHAIN TO KEEP PUBLIC DATA PUBLIC

by Brian Forde

A few months after he took office, President Trump's administration made a change to the White House website. The site's digital updates are often small and insignificant—updating a photo, fixing a broken link—and therefore may go unnoticed. But this one was different, and it could have an impact on every single American. The update eliminated the White House's open data.[1]

On the surface, those nine gigabytes of data sets may seem inconsequential: They include White House visitor logs, the titles and salaries of every White House employee, and government budget data. But that information helps to ensure transparency in government. It helps reporters and citizens figure out who has the ear of the president and his staff, for example. In response to this very issue, Democrats introduced the Make Access Records Available to Lead American Government Openness Act, or MAR-A-LAGO Act, legislation that would require the Trump administration to publish visitor logs for the White House and any other location where the president regularly conducts official business.[2]

The Obama administration drastically increased the openness of government data, codifying it with an executive order that made open, machine-readable data the new default for government information, to ensure that we have transparency in government. So, although the Trump administration's move is a return to the opacity of past administrations, it's a move in the wrong direction. Perhaps most important is what this could mean for the U.S. government's entire open data strategy, as the administration controls the information that so many businesses, organizations, and individual Americans depend on daily.

If you checked the weather this morning, you relied on information that was supplied by government open data. Used GPS to get to a meeting? That information was supplied by government open data. Received an alert that the baby crib you purchased was recalled? That, too, was supplied by government open data.

Unfortunately, it's not just the Trump administration that has been caught deleting or altering important data. Companies are doing it too. Volkswagen cheated on emissions tests.[3] Uber showed fake information about available drivers to government employees. And Airbnb was caught purging more than 1,000 listings, which were in violation of New York state law, just before it shared its data with the public as part of a pledge "to build an open and transparent community."[4]

Data is under attack. And it is the leaders of governments and economies who are waging this war. They have made it acceptable to manipulate raw data in a way that benefits them financially or politically—and it has lowered public confidence in the veracity of information. These are institutions we rely on every day to make the policy and business decisions that affect our economy and society at large. If anyone is allowed to simply change a number or delete a data set, who—and what—are citizens supposed to believe? How can we get our data back?

The answer lies with the public—public blockchains, to be specific.

A public blockchain, like the one bitcoin uses, is a ledger that keeps time-stamped records of every transaction.

Recording a transaction on a public blockchain is the digital equivalent of writing something in stone—it's permanent. More important, it's publicly available for anyone to see and verify.

The first public blockchain was conceived of as a way to record financial transactions, but people have started using it as a way to time-stamp the existence of digital files, such as documents or images. The public blockchain establishes that a specific person or entity had possession of a file at a specific date and time. Useful for patent or copyright claims, the blockchain could also ensure that a government agency or company verifiably published its data—and allow the public to access and confirm that the file they have is the same one that was signed and time-stamped by the creator.

The time stamp and signature alone don't prove that the data is accurate, of course. Other forms of checks and balances, such as comparing data against tax or SEC filings, can be added to ensure that there are legal ramifications for entities that manipulate their data. In the same way, government data, like employment or climate data, could be checked against local, state, or academically collected information that has already been time-stamped and signed by credible institutions.

Using the public blockchain in this manner would not only address our data access and manipulation issues but also lay the groundwork for a better system to more efficiently and effectively regulate the fastest-moving startups. Some tech companies, with their near-instantaneous feedback loops, believe they can regulate their ecosystems more efficiently and effectively than governments can, with their antiquated, in-person inspection efforts. And there's some truth to that. Right now, many local and state governments regulate ride sharing and home sharing in ways similar to how they regulate taxis and hotels, with a combination of police officers, signs, and consumer complaints through 3-1-1 calls. At the same time, governments have watched these startups manipulate their data, and are therefore reticent to trust a company that might put its financial motivations ahead of regulation.

With each party wary of the other's motives and practices, it's been difficult to settle on a compromise. But if governments and emerging technology companies used the public blockchain, both parties could achieve what they want. Companies could move fast, and consumer safety and rights would be protected.

As respected venture capitalist and author Tim O'Reilly says, "Regulations, which specify how to execute laws in much more detail, should be regarded in much the same way that programmers regard their code and algorithms—that is, as a constantly updated tool set to achieve the outcomes specified in the laws."[5]

Conceivably, companies would update their information to the blockchain, with secure mechanisms put in place to protect individual and corporate privacy, and the government would use this data, submitted in real time, to apply local laws to those companies, their employees or contractors, and consumers. The government agency responsible for overseeing the industry would then analyze data, such as consumer feedback ratings and other relevant information (for example, whether ride-sharing drivers take tourists on a longer route), to improve safety and better protect the rights of everyone involved. In other words, the government would use lightweight algorithmic regulation to protect local citizen rights and safety.

The public blockchain would fundamentally change the way we govern and do business. Rather than asking companies and consumers to downgrade their digital interactions in order to comply with the law, the government would create an adaptable system that would reduce the amount of paperwork and compliance for businesses and consumers. Rather than force emerging technologies and business models into legal gray areas, the government would use algorithmic regulation to create a level playing field for incumbent companies in their respective industries.

Unless we tackle our crisis of data now, distrust between government, businesses, and citizens will reach an untenable peak. The growth and innovation of our startup economy will be stunted, and the ability for local and state governments to effectively govern will simply erode. We need open data to keep making important business and policy decisions—and we need to put it back into the hands of the public. Our data problem doesn't have to be a crisis. It can be an opportunity—a chance for our business leaders and policy makers to rebuild a foundation of trust in the critical data we all depend on.

TAKEAWAYS

The leaders of our governments and economies are waging a war on data. They have made it acceptable to manipulate raw data in a way that benefits them financially or politically—and it has lowered public confidence in the veracity of information. Public blockchains could help reverse this.

✓ Recording a transaction on a public blockchain is the digital equivalent of writing something in stone. It's publicly available, permanently, for anyone to see and verify.

✓ Blockchain could also ensure that a government agency or company verifiably published its data—and allow the public to access and confirm that the file they have is the same one that was signed and time-stamped by the creator.

✓ Using the public blockchain in this manner would not only address our data access and manipulation issues but also lay the groundwork for a better system to more efficiently and effectively regulate the fastest-moving startups.

NOTES

1. Tracie Mauriello, "Government Watchdogs Criticize Trump's Removal of Open Data Sets," Government Technology, February 22, 2017, http://www.govtech.com/data/Government -Watchdogs-Criticize-Trumps-Removal-of-Open-Data-Sets.html.

2. Jordain Carney, "Dems Introduce MAR-A-LAGO Act to Publish Visitor Logs," *The Hill*, March 24, 2017, https://thehill.com /blogs/floor-action/senate/325651-dems-introduce-bill-to-publish -mar-a-lago-white-house-visitor-logs?amp.

3. Jeffrey Liker, "Assessing the Sins of Volkswagen, Toyota, and General Motors," hbr.org, September 24, 2015, https://hbr.org/2015 /09/assessing-the-sins-of-volkswagen-toyota-and-general-motors.

4. Jonah Engel Bromwich, "Airbnb Purged New York Listings to Create a Rosier Portrait, Report Says," *New York Times*, February 11, 2016, https://www.nytimes.com/2016/02/12/business

/airbnb-purged-new-york-listings-to-create-a-rosier-portrait
-report-says.html.

5. Tim O'Reilly, "Chapter 22: Open Data and Algorithmic Regulation," *Beyond Transparency*, https://beyondtransparency.org
/chapters/part-5/open-data-and-algorithmic-regulation/.

Adapted from content posted on hbr.org, originally published March 31, 2017 (product #H03JGL).

16

BLOCKCHAIN WILL HELP US PROVE OUR IDENTITIES IN A DIGITAL WORLD

by Michael Mainelli

Who are you?" may well be the world's most frequently asked question. On a website, in a nightclub, at an airport, or in front of a bank counter, everyone wants us to prove that we are who we say we are.

But 2.4 billion poor people worldwide, about 1.5 billion of whom are over the age of 14, can't answer that question to the satisfaction of authorities. While *they* certainly know who they are, they are often excluded from property ownership, free movement, and social protection simply because they can't prove their identity. They are more exposed to corruption and crime, including people trafficking and slavery. (Insightfully, the United Nations is aiming to change this, with UN Sustainable Development Goal #16, Peace, Justice, and Strong Institutions, aiming to "provide legal identity to all, including birth registration, by 2030.")

Globalization and population growth increase the pressure to find cost-effective solutions to prove identity. Recent advances in biometrics, from iris scanning to DNA analysis and voice pattern recognition, are likely to play an important technical role in fixing this, yet identity is not necessarily something that *is* fixed. Our identities are records of our past behavior, and they change over time. Our identities can also vary depending on who is doing the identifying. For example, the tax office probably has little interest in your school report cards but may care enormously about the days you spent out of the country as an adult.

Proof of identity can be a problem for rich and poor alike. For the rich, regulations around anti-money laundering, know-your-customer, and ultimate beneficial ownership increase legal and regulatory costs and hassles. Ninety percent of businesses responding to the International Chamber of Commerce's 2016 Global Survey on Trade Finance pointed to anti-money laundering as the most significant impediment to trade.

For the poor, Hernando de Soto, the Peruvian economist famous for his work on the informal economy, observes: "Without an integrated formal property system, a modern market economy is inconceivable."[1] Thus a modern market economy is inconceivable without proper identification, because there are no proven holders of property rights.

While hassles for the wealthy are a world away from the daily toils of the "great undocumented," the solution to their problems may be the same: mutual distributed ledgers (MDLs), or blockchain technology. MDLs are unalterable registers that allow groups of people to validate, record, and track transactions across a network of decentralized computer systems. The computers follow a common protocol that allows individuals to add new transactions and distribute them using peer-to-peer architecture. MDLs are multiorganizational databases with a super audit trail. Whereas a central database can lead to a natural monopoly that everyone has to use, the fact that MDLs are mutual—that is, held in common—means they are hard to exploit as natural monopolies. You can't charge me for my copy of the ledger, because you don't own it. No one does.

A common question after two decades of MDLs is "What is the killer app?" Since the 2009 launch of bitcoin, the short and somewhat shaky answer has been cryptocurrencies. Bitcoin has had its ups and downs. It stirs up economic controversy with its community's libertarian "new currency" agenda and high price volatility. Bitcoin also stirs up social controversy as rumors of heavy criminal trading of drugs and guns rightly attracts the attention of law enforcement agencies. Yet this decentralized cryptocurrency and its underlying MDL technology works, and some regulators grudgingly allow financial firms to use it.

Now a more fundamental killer app for MDLs is emerging: the secure storage and transmission of digitally signed documents with a super audit trail. These immutable document exchange networks are emerging in trade finance, shipping, and insurance, where everyone has a big problem validating the identity of people and assets. An identity document exchange typically has three parties: (1) the subject, which is an individual or an asset, (2) the certifier, which is usually an organization that notarizes documents, like a government agency, an accounting firm, or a credit referencing agency, and (3) the inquisitor, which is an organization conducting know-your-customer/anti-money-laundering (KYC/AML) checks on the subject.

Typically, there are two distinct MDLs: a content ledger holding the individually encrypted documents, and a transaction ledger holding encryption key access on a series of "key rings," which are folders for documents such as identity, health, or academic qualifications. The subject can give the identity certifier permission to put digitally certified documents on the subject's key rings. For example, a law firm might provide digitally signed copies of documents it has notarized to the subject for them to keep and use. A government might provide each of us with a digitally signed copy of our driving license for us to control. Certifiers have no further access to the data, but inquisitors rely on the data being stamped by a trusted third party, much as a notary public notarizes a physical document.

The subject gives controlled key usage to inquisitors to inspect the documents with smart contracts, pieces of code recorded on the MDL. The network can restrict the number or timing of inquisitions and record them all for the subject. Third parties such as banks, insurers, or governments can get permission to access documents based on the permissions framework coded into the MDL. Commercial certifiers, such as accountants, lawyers, or notaries, may provide indemnities, such as insurance of validity, to inquisitors for a fee.

Tellingly, since 2007 Estonia has been operating a universal national digital identity scheme in which all government data about individuals is stored on a distributed ledger that individuals control and can pass to others.

This digital identity system powers a low-paperwork society using digital signatures. The scheme is so useful that nonnationals use it for their personal digital signatures elsewhere in Europe.

Both high-net-worth and low-net-worth customers expect to have a sensible, inexpensive, global way to prove their identity, whether it is for payments, credit, government records, health records, or academic qualifications. MDL technology is ideally suited for immutable identity document exchange networks, and there are many initiatives under way to realize their potential. Empowering individuals to store, update, and manage access to their data seems rather obvious, including exercising their "right to be forgotten" by canceling their keys.

Proving your identity today is an expensive process. Each identity document validation takes a lot of time and uses low-tech paperwork. People would like to get more use from expensively validated identity documents. One way is to increase the number of uses. For example, in Estonia, banks realized that account access could be given on the national ID as well as a bank card. The rise of many-use IDs could in turn drive consolidation toward a few competitive global systems.

But this is no panacea. The ultimate question surrounding an immutable identity ledger is this: Will it become a lifeline for people, or a burden? Using ledgers that never lose data could materially alter the way society views identity, privacy, and security. Bureaucratic slips such as a mistyped name can be corrected, but the slip can never be forgotten. Behaviors will change, and societal conventions will alter as a result. For example, we may be more tolerant of other people's histories when they can see our own unpaid fines or misdemeanors. Perhaps we will be more intrusive with important issues such as lying about academic qualifications, and more forgiving with lighter matters such as a few mediocre grades.

And think of our permanent legacies. Perhaps we will act more responsibly if our legacy is indelible. For example, we might choose to donate our health data to research through smart contracts triggered by our death certificates. When our identities are forever etched in immutable stone, "Don't you forget about me" may prove to be a more enduring tune than we ever could have imagined.

TAKEAWAYS

Proof of identity can be a problem for rich and poor alike. Blockchain may be able to provide a sensible, inexpensive, global way to prove their identity, whether for payments, credit, government records, health records, or academic qualifications.

✓ Mutual distributed ledgers can be used for the secure storage and transmission of digitally signed documents with a super audit trail. These immutable document exchange networks are emerging in trade finance, shipping, and insurance, where everyone struggles to validate the identity of people and assets.

✓ The ultimate question surrounding an immutable identity ledger is this: Will it become a lifeline for people, or a burden? Using ledgers that never lose data could materially alter the way society views identity, privacy, and security.

NOTE

1. Hernando De Soto, *The Mystery of Capital: Why Capitalism Triumphs in the West and Fails Everywhere Else* (New York: Basic Books, 2003), p. 164.

Adapted from content posted on hbr.org, originally published March 16, 2017 (product #H03JA8).

MAKING CRYPTOCURRENCY MORE ENVIRONMENTALLY SUSTAINABLE

by Marc Blinder

B lockchain has the power to change our world for the better in so many ways. It can provide unbanked people with digital wallets, prevent fraud, and re-place outdated systems with more efficient ones. But we still need this new and improved world to be one that we want to live in. The largest cryptocurrencies—bitcoin, bitcoin cash, and Ethereum—require vast amounts of energy consumption to function. In 2017, blockchain used more power than 159 individual nations including Uruguay, Nigeria, and Ireland.[1] Unsurprisingly, this is creating a huge environmental problem that poses a threat to the Paris Agreement.

It's a brutal, if unintended, consequence for such a promising technology, and "mining" is at the heart of the problem. When bitcoin was first conceived nearly a decade ago, it was a niche fascination for a few hundred hobbyists, or "miners." Because bitcoin has no bank to regulate it, miners used their computers to verify transactions by solving cryptographic problems, similar to complex math problems. Then, they combined the verified transactions into "blocks" and added them to the blockchain (a public record of all the transactions) to document them—all this, in return for a small sum of bitcoin. But where a single bitcoin once sold for less than a penny on the open market, it now sells for nearly $7,000, and around 200,000 bitcoin transactions occur every day. With these numbers increasing, so has the incentive to create cryptocurrency "mines"—server farms now spread across the world, often massive. Imagine the amount of energy consumed by 25,000 machines calculating math problems 24 hours a day.

Beyond the environmental concerns, this inefficiency threatens blockchain as a meaningful platform for enterprise. The high energy costs are baked into the system, and, because the cost of running the network is passed on in transaction fees, users of these networks end up paying for them. Initially, companies that use bitcoin may not see the financial consequences, but as they scale, the costs could become fatal.

The good news: There are a variety of alternatives available that can help organizations cut massive energy costs. Right now, they aren't being adopted quickly enough. Companies that want to keep their heads above water—along with everyone else's—need to educate themselves. Below are two areas that are a good place to start.

Green Energy Blockchain Mining

An immediate fix is mining with solar power and other green energy sources. Each day, Texas alone receives more solar power than we need to replace every nonsolar power plant in the world. There are numerous commercial services for powering crypto mining on server farms that only use clean, renewable energy. Genesis Mining, for instance, enables mining for bitcoin and Ethereum in the cloud. The Iceland-based company uses 100%

renewable energy and is now among the largest miners in the world.

We need to incentivize green energy for future blockchains, too. Every company that uses blockchain also defines its own system for miner compensation. New blockchains could easily offer miners better incentives, like more cryptocurrency, for using green energy—eventually forcing out polluting miners. They could also require all miners to prove that they use green energy and deny payment to those who don't.

Energy-Efficient Blockchain Systems

While bitcoin, bitcoin cash, and Ethereum all depend on energy-inefficient cryptographic problem solving known as "proof of work" to operate, many newer blockchains use "proof-of-stake" (PoS) systems that rely on market incentives. Server owners on PoS systems are called "validators"—not "miners." They put down a deposit, or "stake," a large amount of cryptocurrency, in exchange for the right to add blocks to the blockchain. In proof-of-work systems, miners compete with each other to see who can solve problems the fastest in exchange for a reward, taking up a large amount of energy. But in PoS systems, validators are chosen by an algorithm that takes their stake into account. Removing the element of competition saves energy and allows each machine in a PoS system to work on one problem at a time, as opposed to a proof-of-work system, in which a plethora of machines are rushing to solve the same problem. Additionally, if a validator fails to behave honestly, they may be removed from the network—which helps keep PoS systems accurate.

Particularly promising is the delegated-proof-of-stake (DPoS) system, which operates somewhat like a representative democracy. In DPoS systems, everyone who has cryptocurrency tokens can vote on which servers become block producers and manage the blockchain as a whole. However, there is one downside. DPoS is somewhat less censorship resistant than proof-of-work systems. Because it only has 21 block producers, in theory, the network could be brought to a stop by simultaneous subpoenas or cease and desist orders, making it more vulnerable to the thousands upon thousands of nodes on Ethereum. But DPoS has proven to be vastly faster at processing transactions while using less energy, and that's a trade-off we in the industry should be willing to make.

Among the largest cryptocurrencies, Ethereum is already working on a transition to PoS, and we should take more collective action to hasten this movement. Developers need to think long and hard before creating new proof-of-work blockchains, because the more successful they become, the worse the ecological impact they may have. Imagine if car companies had been wise enough, several decades ago, to come together and set emission standards for themselves. It would have helped cultivate a healthier planet—and preempted billions of dollars in costs when those standards were finally imposed on them. The blockchain industry is now at a similar inflection point. The question is whether we'll be wiser than the world-changing industries that came before us.

TAKEAWAYS

The largest cryptocurrencies require vast amounts of energy consumption to function. In 2017, blockchain used more power than 159 individual nations including Uruguay, Nigeria, and Ireland. This is creating a huge environmental problem that poses a threat to the Paris Agreement.

✓ With the value of cryptocurrency increasing, so has the incentive to create "mines"—massive server farms spread across the world, calculating math problems 24 hours a day.

✓ A variety of alternatives are available that can help organizations cut massive energy costs associated with blockchain, but they aren't being adopted quickly enough.

✓ An immediate fix is mining with solar power and other green energy sources. Every company that uses blockchain also defines its own system for miner compensation. New blockchains could easily offer miners better incentives for using green energy.

✓ Blockchains that use a proof-of-stake system rather than a proof-of-work system are less energy-intensive. If the blockchain industry can make the hard choice to adopt greener decisions now, it may avoid having green standards forced upon it in the future.

NOTE

1. "Bitcoin Energy Consumption Index," Digiconomist, https://digiconomist.net/bitcoin-energy-consumption.

Adapted from content posted on hbr.org, originally published November 27, 2018 (product #H04O38).

About the Contributors

ROBLEH ALI is a research scientist at the MIT Digital Currency Initiative.

ALLISON BERKE is the executive director of the Stanford Cyber Initiative.

MARC BLINDER is chief product officer of blockchain-based startup AIKON. He developed a social network called MobilePlay (sold to Good Technology) and held leadership roles at Context Optional and Efficient Frontier (sold to Adobe). Follow him on Twitter @mblinder.

MICHAEL J. CASEY is the author of *The Age of Cryptocurrency: How Bitcoin and the Blockchain Are Challenging the Global Economic Order.* He is a senior adviser at the MIT Media Lab's Digital Currency Initiative and a partner with Agentic Group.

CHRISTIAN CATALANI is the Fred Kayne (1960) Career Development Professor of Entrepreneurship and Assistant

Professor of Technological Innovation, Entrepreneurship, and Strategic Management at the MIT Sloan School of Management. Christian is one of the principal investigators of the MIT Digital Currencies Research Study, which gave all MIT undergraduate students access to bitcoin in 2014.

PRIMAVERA DE FILIPPI is a permanent researcher at the National Center of Scientific Research (CNRS) in Paris. She is faculty associate at the Berkman Klein Center for Internet & Society at Harvard Law School, where she is investigating the concept of "governance-by-design" as it relates to online distributed architectures.

ANTONIO FATÁS is a professor at INSEAD. He is also a research fellow at the Centre for Economic and Policy Research in London, England.

BRIAN FORDE is senior lecturer for bitcoin and blockchain at the MIT Sloan School of Management. He was senior adviser for mobile and data innovation in the Obama White House and cofounded one of the largest phone companies in Nicaragua after serving in the U.S. Peace Corps. Brian was named a Young Global Leader and one of the 10 most influential people in bitcoin and blockchain by the World Economic Forum.

VINAY GUPTA is the founder of Hexayurt Capital, a fund that invests in creating the Internet of Agreements. He was instrumental in creating the Dubai Blockchain Strategy, project-managed the Ethereum blockchain platform release and invented the hexayurt refugee shelter.

CAMPBELL R. HARVEY is professor of finance and the J. Paul Sticht Professor of International Business at the Fuqua School of Business, Duke University. He served as the 2016 president of the American Finance Association. He is investment strategy adviser to Man Group, PLC, and partner and senior adviser to Research Affiliates, LLC.

MARCO IANSITI is the David Sarnoff Professor of Business Administration at Harvard Business School, where he heads the Technology and Operations Management Unit and the Digital Initiative. He has advised many companies in the technology sector, including Microsoft, Facebook, and Amazon.

JOICHI ITO is the director of the MIT Media Lab and MIT professor of the practice in media arts and sciences.

KARIM R. LAKHANI is the Charles Edward Wilson Professor of Business Administration and the Dorothy and Michael Hintze Fellow at Harvard Business School. He is also the founding director of the Harvard Innovation Science Laboratory.

MICHAEL MAINELLI is executive chairman of Z/Yen Group. Z/Yen has been working with mutual distributed ledgers since 1995. His book, *The Price of Fish: A New Approach to Wicked Economics and Better Decisions*, written with Ian Harris, won the 2012 Independent Publisher Book Awards' Finance, Investment & Economics Gold Prize.

CHRISTINE MOORMAN is the T. Austin Finch, Sr. Professor of Business Administration at Duke University's Fuqua School of Business and the editor-in-chief designate of the *Journal of Marketing*.

PATRICK MURCK is a fellow at the Berkman Klein Center for Internet & Society at Harvard University, where he works on the Digital Finance Initiative and conducts research into the law and policy implications of blockchains, smart contracts, and financial technology. In addition, Patrick is special counsel at Cooley, a global law firm, as part of the financial technology team. He has been recognized as one of "America's 50 Outstanding General Counsel" by the *National Law Journal* and is a member of the IMF's High-Level Advisory Group on FinTech.

NEHA NARULA is director of research at the MIT Digital Currency Initiative.

STEPHEN J. OBIE is a partner at Jones Day and a leader of the firm's blockchain initiative.

YUDAN PANG is a marketing PhD student at Harbin Institute of Technology.

MARK W. RASMUSSEN is a partner at Jones Day and a leader of the firm's blockchain initiative.

ALEX TAPSCOTT is founder and CEO of Northwest Passage Ventures, a consultancy, advisory firm, and investor in the blockchain industry. He is a coauthor of *Blockchain Revolution: How the Technology Behind Bitcoin Is Changing Money, Business and the World*. Follow him on Twitter @alextapscott.

DON TAPSCOTT is the bestselling author of *Wikinomics*, *The Digital Economy*, and a dozen other acclaimed books about technology, business, and society. According to Thinkers50, Don is the fourth most important living management thinker in the world; he is an adjunct professor at the Rotman School of Management, and chancellor of Trent University. He and his son Alex are coauthors of *Blockchain Revolution: How the Technology Behind Bitcoin Is Changing Money, Business, and the World*. Follow him on Twitter @dtapscott.

MARC TOLEDO is a senior associate at PwC focusing on blockchain and digital transformation. In his previous work at the World Bank and Apple, he led large projects related to cybersecurity, machine learning, and artificial intelligence.

CATHERINE TUCKER is the Distinguished Professor of Management Science at MIT Sloan School of Management.

BEATRICE WEDER DI MAURO is the Chaired Professor of Economic Policy and International Macroeconomics at the University of Mainz in Germany. She is also a Fellow at the Emerging Markets Institute of INSEAD and a research fellow at the Centre for Economic Policy Research in London, England.

PINDAR WONG is the chairman of VeriFi Ltd., a discreet internet financial infrastructure consultancy and founder of OBOR.IO, which pioneered the "Belt and Road Blockchain." He is a bitcoin protocol enthusiast and chairs ScalingBitcoin.org.

Index

Is Your Business Ready for the Future?

If you enjoyed this book and want more on today's pressing business topics, turn to other books in the **Insights You Need** series from *Harvard Business Review*. Featuring HBR's latest thinking on topics critical to your company's success—from Blockchain and Cybersecurity to AI and Agile—each book will help you explore these trends and how they will impact you and your business in the future.

FOR MORE VISIT HBR.ORG/BOOKS

The most important management ideas all in one place.

We hope you enjoyed this book from *Harvard Business Review*. Now you can get even more with HBR's 10 Must Reads Boxed Set. From books on leadership and strategy to managing yourself and others, this 6-book collection delivers articles on the most essential business topics to help you succeed.

HBR's 10 Must Reads Series

The definitive collection of ideas and best practices on our most sought-after topics from the best minds in business.

- Change Management
- Collaboration
- Communication
- Emotional Intelligence
- Innovation
- Leadership
- Making Smart Decisions

- Managing Across Cultures
- Managing People
- Managing Yourself
- Strategic Marketing
- Strategy
- Teams
- The Essentials

hbr.org/mustreads

Buy for your team, clients, or event.
Visit hbr.org/bulksales for quantity discount rates.